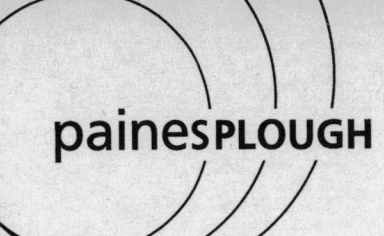

paines**PLOUGH**

D0188712

Pyrenees
by David Greig

Cast

The Man	Hugh Ross
Vivienne	Paola Dionisotti
Anna	Frances Grey
The Proprietor	Jonathan McGuinness
Director	Vicky Featherstone
Designer	Neil Warmington
Lighting Designer	Natasha Chivers
Original Music & Sound	Nick Powell
Production Manager	Jo Masson
Deputy Stage Manager	David Young
Technical Stage Manager	Mat Ort

Press Representatives

Emma Schad 07930 308018
(for Paines Plough)

Ann Nugent 07900 372702
(for the Tron)

Cover Image

Stuart McCaffer
lostdug@hotmail.com

First performed at the Tron Theatre, Glasgow 9th March 2005

The playscript that follows was correct at time of going to press,
but may have changed during rehearsal.

DAVID GREIG
Writer

David Greig was born in Edinburgh. For Paines Plough: The Cosmonaut's Last Message To The Woman He Once Loved In The Former Soviet Union. Other plays include: Europe, The Architect, The Speculator, Victoria, Outlying Islands, San Diego, When the Bulbul Stopped Singing. His work with the theatre company Suspect Culture includes: One Way Street, Airport, Timeless, Mainstream, Casanova, Lament and 8000 Miles. David's translation of Caligula was presented at the Donmar Warehouse in an award winning production in 2003. His work for children and young people includes: Danny 306+Me Forever and Dr Korczak's Example. David has also written extensively for radio.

NATASHA CHIVERS
Lighting Design

During This Other England Natasha is designing: The Small Things, Mercury Fur, Pyrenees and If Destroyed True. For Paines Plough: The Straits (with Drum Theatre Plymouth & Hampstead Theatre inc. New York tour), On Blindness (with Frantic Assembly & Graeae), The Drowned World, Tiny Dynamite (with Frantic Assembly inc. International Tour). Theatre includes: Urban Legend and The Kindness Of Strangers (Liverpool Everyman 40th anniversary Season), Who's Afraid Of The Big Bad Book? (Soho Theatre), Ma Rainey's Black Bottom and The Entertainer (Liverpool Playhouse), Very Little Women (Lip Service tour), Hymns (Frantic Assembly/Lyric Hammersmith), The Bomb-itty of Errors (The New Ambassadors/Dublin), The Cherry Orchard and After The Dance (Oxford Stage Company), Playhouse Creatures (West Yorkshire Playhouse), Peepshow (Frantic Assembly, Plymouth Theatre Royal, Lyric Hammersmith), Sell Out (Frantic Assembly), Wit and The Memory Of Water (Stellar Quines), Present Laughter (Bath Theatre Royal Productions).

VICKY FEATHERSTONE
Director

Vicky Featherstone is currently Artistic Director of the National Theatre of Scotland. While Artistic Director of Paines Plough she directed: On Blindness by Glyn Cannon, The Drowned World by Gary Owen (Pearson Best Play, Fringe First), Tiny Dynamite by Abi Morgan (MEN Best Fringe Production), Crazy Gary's Mobile Disco by Gary Owen, Splendour by Abi Morgan (TMA/Barclays Best Director & Best Play, Fringe First & Herald Angel), Riddance by Linda McLean, (Fringe First & Herald Angel), The Cosmonaut's Last Message To The Woman He Once Loved In The Former Soviet Union by David Greig, Crave by Sarah Kane, Sleeping Around by Hilary Fannin, Stephen Greenhorn, Abi Morgan and Mark Ravenhill, and Crazyhorse by Parv Bancil.

PAOLA DIONISOTTI
Vivian

Paola was born in Turin, Italy and trained at the Drama Centre, London. Theatre includes: The Entertainer (Liverpool Playhouse), When We Are Rich (Nuffield Theatre), Further Than The Furthest Thing (Tron Theatre/National Theatre), Drink, Dance, Laugh & Lie (Bush Theatre), Holy Mothers (Royal Court/Ambassador Theatre Company), Camino Real (Young Vic), The Misfits (Royal Exchange, Manchester), The Machine Wreckers, Richard II, Square Rounds, Countrymania, The Wondering Jew (National Theatre), Plays by Gertrude Stein (Citizens), Heresies, Moscow Gold (RSC), The Trojan Woman, Vassa (The Gate), Britannicus (Crucible, Sheffield), Ghosts (Edinburgh Lyceum), On The Verge (Sadlers Wells). Television includes: Minor Complications, Fame is the Spur, The Monocled Mutineer, The House of Elliot, The Gospels, Devil's Advocate, Maisie Rain, Harbour Lights, Spinechillers (BBC), A Fine Romance, The Young Ones (LWT), A Murder is Announced, They Never Do What You Want (Thames), The First Among Equals (Granada), Forever Green, Ruth Rendall - The Veiled One, Just William (ITV), Peak Practice (Central), Fergus' Wedding (RTE). Film includes: The Sailor's Return (BFI), Vigo...A Passion For Life (Impact Nitrate Vigo), The Titchbourne Claimant (Bigger Picture Company), Intimacy (Telema Films), Come & Go (Parallel Films), Loves Brother (Palace Films). In 2003 she directed her first professional production: Two Sisters and a Piano by Nilo Cruz (Tron/Out of the Box Productions).

FRANCES GREY
Anna

Theatre includes: Dark Earth (Traverse), Playhouse Creatures (West Yorkshire Playhouse), Platonov (Almeida), Rebecca, Jekyll and Hyde (Edinburgh Lyceum), The Importance Of Being Earnest (Old Vic). Television includes: The Key (Key Films Ltd), Messiah - 3 series, Murder In Mind, Vanity Fair, Accused, As You Like It "In Rehearsal" (BBC), The Secret Life of Michael Fry (Endor), Reach For The Moon (LWT), Taggart (STV). Film includes: Janice Beard - 45 WPM (Dakota Films), E-Male (Sweet Child Films for Arte), Crimetime (Focus Films).

JONATHAN MCGUINNESS
The Proprietor

For Paines Plough: Crazy Horse. Other theatre includes: Jeff Koons (ATC), A Midsummer Night's Dream, Henry VI (Propeller/ Watermill/ Haymarket Theatre Royal), Richard III, Mojo (Crucible Theatre, Sheffield), Last Valentine (Almeida), Twelfth Night, Comedy Of Errors, Henry V (Propeller/ Watermill Theatre), The Moment Is A Gift (Prada), Two Weeks With The Queen (Leicester Haymarket), The Champion of Paribanou (Stephen Joseph Theatre Company). Television includes: The Catherine Tate Sketch Show (BBC/ Tiger Aspect), A Touch Of Frost (Yorkshire Television), In Search Of The Brontes, Have Your Cake And Eat It (BBC), The Bill (Thames), Coogan's Run (Talkback).

HUGH ROSS
The Man

Hugh was born in Glasgow and studied at Glasgow Academy and St. Andrews University. He trained at the Royal Academy of Dramatic Art. Theatre includes: Love Me Tonight (Hampstead Theatre), The Woman In Black (Fortune Theatre), Hare Trilogy (Birmingham Rep), A Prayer for Owen Meany, Battle Royal, Lady In the Dark (National Theatre), Fifty Revolutions (Whitehall Theatre), Invention of Love (Theatre Royal Haymarket), Passion (Queen's Theatre, London), Tartuffe (Royal Exchange, Manchester), Democracy (Bush Theatre), Dr Faustus, Mary Stuart (Greenwich Theatre), King Lear (Royal Court), Death And The Maiden (Duke of York's), Hedda Gabler (Playhouse Theatre), As You Like It, All's Well That End's Well (RSC), Bussy D'Ambois (The Old Vic), Twelfth Night, The Cid (Cheek By Jowl). Television includes: Mine All Mine (ITV), Sea of Souls, Snoddy, Deal Souls, Cazalet Chronicle, Invasion Earth, Between The Lines, Lovejoy, Absolutely Fabulous, An Ungentlemanly Act, Misterioso (BBC), Men Only (World Productions/ Channel Four), Mists Of Avalon (TNT/ Warner Brothers), Family Money (Whistling Gypsy Productions), Sharpe's Sword, Sharpe's Battle, Sharpe's Gold (Central Films), Taggart, Dr Finlay, The Advocates (STV), Poirot (LWT). Film includes: Charlotte Gray (Ecosse Films), The Four Feathers (Miramax), The Tell-Tale Heart (Telltale Films Ltd.), Gooseberries Don't Dance (Quadriga Productions), Trainspotting (Polygram/ Channel 4), Patriot Games (Paramount British Pictures), Nightbreed (Morgan Creek/ 20th Century Fox). Hugh has also directed: The Glass Menagerie (Tower Theatre), Stevie (Mercury, Colchester), After Liverpool (RSC).

NEIL WARMINGTON
Designer

Neil Graduated in Fine Art Painting from Maidstone College of Art before attending the Motley theatre design course in London. Neil is designing The Small Things, Pyrenees and If Destroyed True, in our This Other England season. For Paines Plough: The Straits, The Drowned World , Splendour, Riddance, Crazy Horse. Other theatre includes: King Lear (ETT/Old Vic), Ghosts, Don Juan, John Gabriel Borkman, Taming of the Shrew, Love's Labours Lost (ETT), Woyzeck, Glass Menagerie, Comedians, Tankred Dorsts Merlin(Royal Lyceum Edinburgh), Full Moon For A Solemn Mass, Family, Passing Places, King of the Fields, Gagarin Way, Slab Boys Trilogy (Traverse/National Theatre), Angels in America (7:84), Life's a Dream, Fiddler on the Roof, Playhouse Creatures, (West Yorkshire Playhouse), Henry V (RSC), Much Ado About Nothing (Queen's London), Sunset Song, Mary Queen of Scots Got Her Head Chopped Off (Theatre Royal, Glasgow) The Life of Stuff (Donmar) Waiting for Godot (Liverpool Everyman), The Tempest (Contact), Jane Eyre, Desire Under the Elms (Shared Experience), Troilus & Cressida (Opera North),Oedipus Rex (Stravinsky) (Connecticut State Opera), The Marriage of Figaro (Garsington Opera), Scenes From An Execution, Dumbstruck, Lie Of The Mind (Dundee) Knives in Hens, The Birthday Party (Tag). Neil has also won three TMA Awards for best design, been part of numerous Edinburgh Fringe first productions and has been awarded The Linbury Prize for stage design, and the Sir Alfred Munnings Florence Prize for painting.

PAINES PLOUGH'S THIS OTHER ENGLAND

at the Menier Chocolate Factory
Friday 28 January – Sunday 22 May 2005.

**"If new writing in this country is going to have any far-reaching
significance, then it needs Paines Plough"**
THE INDEPENDENT

This Other England is a ground-breaking body of work marking the 30th anniversary
of new writing powerhouse Paines Plough.

Taking its cue from Melvyn Bragg's BBC Radio 4 series The Routes of English, Paines
Plough commissioned eight outstanding voices of theatre to think about English as a
language and how it shapes our identity. This season we premiere the first four of
these commissions which offer a theatrical cross-section of where we are now. This is
the start of an extraordinary series, we hope you will join us and be a part of it from
the beginning.

**"Paines Plough remains at the Pinnacle of
New British theatre."** METRO

An exceptional season deserves a great venue and we are proud to be presenting
these productions at London's most inspiring new venue, the Menier Chocolate
Factory, which offers a unique space minutes from London Bridge with an atmospheric
bar and delicious candlelit restaurant.

This season would not have been possible without the vision and commitment of our
co-producing partners. For Mercury Fur; Drum Theatre Plymouth. For Pyrenees; Tron
Theatre Glasgow and in association with Watford Palace Theatre. For If Destroyed
True; Dundee Rep Theatre. Each production is appearing at its associated venue as
well as in London during the season.

THE SMALL THINGS by Enda Walsh
Menier Chocolate Factory, London. Fri 28 Jan - Sun 27 Feb.
MERCURY FUR by Philip Ridley
Drum Theatre Plymouth. Thurs 10 Feb - Sat 26 Feb.
Menier Chocolate Factory, London. Tues 1 Mar - Sun 27 Mar.
PYRENEES by David Greig
Tron Theatre, Glasgow. Wed 9 Mar - Sat 26 Mar.
Menier Chocolate Factory, London. Tues 29 Mar - Sun 24 Apr.
Watford Palace Theatre. Tues 26 Apr - Sat 30 Apr.
IF DESTROYED TRUE by Douglas Maxwell
Dundee Rep Theatre. Sat 9 Apr - Sat 23 Apr.
Menier Chocolate Factory, London. Tues 26 Apr - Sun 22 May.

Supported by the Peggy Ramsay Foundation

PAINES PLOUGH PRESENTS... ENGAGE

Engage: Take part, participate, involve (a person or his or her attention), intensely, employ (a person), begin a battle with, bring (a mechanism) into operation.

engage: Wild Lunch Funsize
Paines Plough and Half MoonYoung People's Theatre are developing short plays for little people by grown up writers - Jennifer Farmer, Dennis Kelly, Abi Morgan, Chloe Moss, Gary Owen and Mark Ravenhill. Performances will be at lunchtime on Tues 22 Mar,Wed 23 Mar, Thurs 24 Mar, Thurs 31 Mar, Fri 1 April and Sat 2 April. Find a child under 7 and bring them along. Tickets are available from Half Moon on 020 7709 8900 and tickets@halfmoon.org.uk

engage: Battle
Chaired by Michael Billington. Leading playwrights duel with each other to persuade the audience that their chosen dramatist is the greatest of all time. You decide who wins. Battle commences at 6.30pm on Fri 4 Mar and Fri 29 April. [FREE]

engage: Later
Curated by Mark Ravenhill. A series of surprising, late night theatrical events dotted throughout the season. Mark will be taking his pick of performers and artists and presenting a taste of their latest work. Performances will be post-show on Fri 25 Feb, Fri 25 Mar, Fri 22 Apr and Fri 20 May. [FREE]

engage: Explore
A chance to take a look behind-the-scenes of This Other England - come down to the Chocolate Factory. We will be receiving visitors from 11am – 3pm on Wed 9 Feb and Wed 6 April [FREE]

engage: Discuss
Each post show discussion will feature a contribution from a guest expert. [FREE]

The Small Things	I speak therefore I am	Thurs 17 Feb
Mercury Fur	When Words Lose Meaning	Thurs 17 Mar
Pyrenees	Language and Identity	Thurs 14 Apr
If Destroyed True	Language and Technology	Thurs 12 May

engage: Whispers of Britain
Assistant Director Hamish Pirie in a dynamic theatrical lecture recounts his pilgrimage to take a Chinese whisper around the British Isles. Performances will be at lunchtimes on Thurs 12 and Fri 13 May. [FREE]

engage: Masterclasses
A new series of our successful writers masterclasses will take place during the second half of This Other England. Full details of dates, titles and workshop leaders will be available at the start of the season.

engage: Schools
We will be offering a limited number of workshops for schools to accompany each of the productions. If you would like to find out more about our provision for schools please contact Susannah on 020 72404533.

Free events are not ticketed and seating is limited so please arrive at the venue in plenty of time to ensure your place.

More information on the participants and content of these events will be available nearer to the time. If you would like to be the first to find out more please email Susannah@painesplough.com with 'e-ngage' in the subject line.

PAINES PLOUGH

"The legendary Paines Plough" *Independent*

Paines Plough is an award-winning nationally and internationally renowned touring theatre company, specialising exclusively in the commissioning and development of contemporary playwrights and the production of their work on stage. We tour the work throughout Britain and overseas ensuring the widest possible audience can benefit from it.

We work with both new and experienced writers and develop plays with a ground-breaking and highly respected programme of workshops and readings. In order to inspire new playwrights and find new audiences, we also have a pioneering education and outreach programme which focuses on encouraging people to write.

Our writers are encouraged to be courageous in their work, to challenge our notions of theatre and the society we live in.

Paines Plough was founded in 1974 by director John Adams and playwright David Pownall to commission and tour new plays. At the time it was the only such company in England and quickly became known as The Writers Company, for its commitment to placing the writer at the centre of the company.

Although Paines Plough has changed direction with the vision of each Artistic Director, there has always been a consistency in commissioning the best writers of each generation and touring this work nationally. These include David Pownall, Stephen Jeffreys, Heathcote Williams, Terry Johnson, Tony Marchant, Pam Gems, Mark Ravenhill, Sarah Kane, Abi Morgan, Gary Owen, David Greig, Philip Ridley, Douglas Maxwell, Enda Walsh, Gregory Burke. Many of these writers have received subsequent commissions from national and regional theatres, film and television companies here and abroad.

At the end of 2004 Paines Plough appointed its eighth Artistic Director, Roxana Silbert, she joined the company in January 2005 to lead us into our next exciting phase.

If you would like to be on Paines Plough's free mailing list, please send your details to:

Helen Poole
Paines Plough, 4th Floor, 43 Aldwych, LONDON WC2B 4DN
T + 44 (0) 20 7240 4533
F + 44 (0) 20 7240 4534
office@painesplough.com
www.painesplough.com

Paines Plough is supported by:

ARTS COUNCIL ENGLAND

Paines Plough are:

Artistic Director	Roxana Silbert
General Manager	Kerry Whelan
Associate Director	John Tiffany
Literary Manager	Lucy Morrison
Projects Manager	Susannah Jeffries
Administrator	Helen Poole
Assistant Director (Arts Council England)	Hamish Pirie
Associate Playwright (Arts Council England)	Dennis Kelly
Pearson Writer in Residence	Chloe Moss

Board of Directors:

Roanna Benn, Tamara Cizeika, Giles Croft, David Edwards (Chair),
Chris Elwell (Vice Chair), Fraser Grant, Clare O'Brien, Jenny Sealey.

**Paines Plough would like to thank the following, without whom
This Other England would not have been possible:**

Alan Brodie	Tamara Cizeika
Robert Kent & Blinkhorns	Nick Eliott
Casarotto Ramsay	Joachim Fleury
Carolyn Bonnyman	Alison Richie
Tricia Mahoney	A D Penalver
David James	Kacey Ainsworth
The Agency	David Aukin and Nancy Meckler
Robbie Jarvis	Sheila Reid
Ashley Pharoah	Antoine Dupuy D'Angeal
Kim Oliver	David Bradshaw
Ann Bowen	Miranda Sawyer
Alan Ayckbourn	Trudi Styler
Adam Kenwright Associates	Old Vic New Voices

THE TRON THEATRE COMPANY, GLASGOW

The Tron, since its inception in 1981 and under the respective artistic leaderships of Michael Boyd, Irina Brown and currently Neil Murray, has established itself as one of the most exciting, creative and consistently successful theatre companies in Britain.

A major capital redevelopment completed in 1999 has coincided with an explosion of activity. In 2000, the Tron produced two world premieres of work by Scottish writers: OUR BAD MAGNET by Douglas Maxwell and, in a co-production with the Royal National Theatre, FURTHER THAN THE FURTHEST THING by Zinnie Harris. Of these, the latter premiered at the Edinburgh Festival, winning four major awards before a run at the National, a transfer to the Tricycle Theatre, London and a tour of South Africa.

More recent achievements have included the world premieres of LOVE FREAKS by Iain Heggie and STANDING WAVE by Nicola McCartney, the Scottish premieres THE BEAUTY QUEEN OF LEENANE by Martin McDonagh (directed by Iain Heggie), DEALER'S CHOICE by Patrick Marber (directed by Zinnie Harris) and THE MEMORY OF WATER by Shelagh Stephenson (a co-production with Edinburgh's Stellar Quines), and, as the centrepiece of the Canadian Six Stages Festival, Adrian Osmond's production of John Mighton's POSSIBLE WORLDS.

In 2003, the Tron mounted a hugely successful revival of Chris Hannan's SHINING SOULS – the first ever in the city of the play's setting – a co-production with v.amp Productions which was awarded Best Production in the inaugural Critics' Awards for Theatre in Scotland.

Later that same year, the Tron produced David Greig's SAN DIEGO for the Edinburgh International Festival. Co-directed by the author, the production became a cause célèbre, selling out in both Glasgow and Edinburgh and winning a Herald Angel Award for David Greig.

This success was followed in 2004 when the Tron returned to the Edinburgh International Festival with Anthony Neilson's THE WONDERFUL WORLD OF DISSOCIA. A collaboration with the Theatre Royal Plymouth and EIF, DISSOCIA was also directed by its writer and also collected a Herald Angel, this time for actress Christine Entwisle.

Later in 2005, the Tron, working with Dundee Rep, are to stage David Greig's version of Alfred Jarry's UBU THE KING as part of the Barbican's Young Genius season.

Director	Neil Murray
General Manager	Fred Emden
Business Development Manager	Eleanor Harris
Education and Outreach Manager	Gillian Gourlay
Production Manager	Joe Masson
Stage Manager	Peter Screen
Technical Manager	Malcolm Rogan
Marketing Manager	Charlie Barron
Box Office Manager	Kathryn Bradley
Front of House Manager	Jim Davidson
Bar and Catering Manager	Morven Stewart

And all the staff of the Tron Theatre, Glasgow.

Tron Theatre, 63 Trongate, Glasgow, G1 5HB
0141 552 3748
www.tron.co.uk

WATFORD PALACE THEATRE

Watford Palace Theatre re-opened in September 2004 following a major £8.7m lottery funded refurbishment, which saw improvements to the foyer and auditorium areas in addition to increased technical capabilities backstage.

Watford Palace Theatre aims to be a national flagship for artistic, cultural and education provision and focus for creativity for people in Watford, Hertfordshire and beyond. The Theatre's purpose is to create theatre made in Watford of the highest quality and innovation that will excite, delight and inspire...

This is created through the partnership between our audiences and the continued support of our funders – Arts Council England East, Watford Borough Council and Hertfordshire County Council; Children, Schools and Families.

The Palace Theatre has always presented dynamic new plays, attracted the most exciting actors and created work with high standards of performance, direction and design. There has been a tremendous diversity within our programming choices and the audiences have remained loyal and enthusiastic. Many of the attendances for new plays exceed those for more familiar plays.

Much of the company's work has been presented across the country. Our co-produced work with companies in Birmingham, Bath, Cambridge, Northampton and Manchester has created positive and meaningful relationships with other producing theatres, including those in our region.

Artistic Director	Lawrence Till
Executive Director	Mary Caws
Literary Director	Joyce Branagh
Head of Finance	Lucy Williams
Head of Sales and Marketing	Craig Titley
Production Manager	Alison Fellows
Theatre Manager	Kate McCarthy
Development Manager	Jane Foy
Associate Director (Active)	Kirstie Davis

Watford Palace Theatre, Clarendon Road, Watford, WD17 1JZ.
Administration 01923 235455 Box Office 01923 225671
www.watfordtheatre.co.uk

David Greig
Pyrenees

faber and faber

First published in 2005
by Faber and Faber Limited
3 Queen Square London WC1N 3AU

Typeset by Country Setting, Kingsdown, Kent CT14 8ES
Printed in England by Mackays of Chatham plc, Chatham, Kent

A CIP record for this book
is available from the British Library

ISBN 0–571–22850–X

2 4 6 8 10 9 7 5 3 1

In memory of Morag Hood

Characters

The Man
Anna
The Proprietor
Vivienne

PYRENEES

We should have been galloping on horses, their
   hoofprints
Splashes of light, divots kicked out of the darkness,
Or hauling up lobster pots in a wake of sparks. Where
Were the otters and seals? Were the dolphins on fire?
Yes, we should have been doing more with our lives.

Michael Longley, 'Water Burn'

Act One

Anna and The Man are seated at a table on the terrace.
   *A mini-cassette recorder sits on the table between
them.*
   *Anna is dressed smartly, for work, but with a nod to
the unusual location of the interview and the season.*
   The Man is wearing a borrowed suit without a tie.

Anna loads the machine with a cassette.
   *She spends an awkwardly long period of time trying to
get it to work.*
   She consults a little folded instruction leaflet.
   She's a little nervous.
   The Man watches her.

Anna It's OK.

The Man Would you –?

Anna No. I've used this machine before.

The Man Sometimes they're temperamental.

Anna Mm.

The Man Would you like –?

Anna I think I've got it.

The Man Good.

   Anna tries the machine.
      It seems to work.

Anna Instructions in five languages, none of it makes any
sense.

The smallest of laughs from Anna.
Something of a pause as she fiddles with it.

The Man There's no rush.

She rewinds.
She presses play.
The recorded voice is distant, barely audible.
The laugh is audible.

Tape: 'Instructions in five languages, none of it makes any sense.'
The smallest of laughs.

She switches it off.
The Man is smiling.

Anna Right.
. . .
I know.
I'm terrible with . . . equipment.
Cars. Things that have a manual.

The Man I'm not laughing at you, honestly.

Anna It's funny.
I deserve it.

The Man No.

Anna Anything mechanical – I get a bit – (*She makes a hand-gesture which seems to conjure clumsy indecisive hands dealing with a small, technical object. Simultaneously she is searching for a word.*) – you know . . . spazzy.

The Man I'm sorry?

Anna I shouldn't really use that word, but you know what I mean.

The Man Spazzy?

Anna It's a bad habit. You don't need to tell me.

The Man I've never heard it before.

Anna Oh.
It's just a childish . . . at school they used to . . .
Really?

The Man It sounds American.

Anna No, it's – it's – gosh –
It's from – I don't even like to say it – spastic. It's –

The Man Spazzy.

Anna But actually it's quite offensive.

The Man Spazzy. (*He laughs.*)

Anna It's not really appropriate any more.

The Man It's a funny word.

Anna At school – it was just – but kids do, don't they?
So – because I'm epileptic.
'Spazzy Anna'.
I just picked it up.
So I should know better, actually.

The Man 'Spazzy Anna'.

Anna Actually really I shouldn't have said it.
Would you mind not mentioning it to anybody?

The Man Not at all.

Anna It's a slight breach of guidelines, you know. That's all.
Anyway – we'll get started.
I don't want to keep you too long.

The Man Keep me as long as you like.
It's a glorious morning.
It's nice to have company.

Anna Yes.

The Man Since my experience, Miss Edwards –

Anna Call me Anna.

The Man Anna – the smallest things seem –

Anna Let's be informal.
   Sorry.

The Man It's quite all right.

Anna The smallest things.

The Man The smallest things –
   You know, a bird or the way a person plays chess.
   They seem part of – I do understand that this is
embarrassing for people – a greater one-ness.
   I feel awake to the wonder of being alive and amongst
things.
   So unfortunately I smile at people more than I should.
   In fact,
   It was your laugh which made me smile.
   Hearing your laugh on the tape.
   That's all.

Anna It's all right. Really.

The Man I probably seem a bit 'spazzy'.

Anna Not at all.

The Man Pay no attention.

Anna No I – it's – actually.
   I know exactly what you mean.
   . . .
   OK.
   Let's . . . so . . . if you could just say something. For a
level.

   She switches the tape on.
   She stands the recorder on the table between them.

The Man . . .

Anna What did you have for breakfast this morning?

The Man I had an English breakfast. Bacon, eggs, sausage, tomato.
Just the usual.

Anna I had the continental.

The Man I dithered over the continental, but in the end I plumped for the English.

Anna OK, that should do.

> *She rewinds the tape a little.*
> *Plays it.*
> *Both listen.*

> *Tape: '. . . dithered over the continental, but in the end I plumped for the English.'*

The Man Do I sound like that?

Anna Yes.

The Man It's strange.

Anna It's always horrible hearing your own voice on tape.

The Man I suppose so.

Anna Does it trigger anything for you? Any memories?

The Man It sounds like –
It's softly spoken.
It's quite a softly spoken voice.
That's all I could say about it.

Anna When I was an actress, I had a voice coach once, and she told me that people carry a landscape in their voice. This was to help us find the right accent. She said that, you know, if a person's from Glasgow their voice would be low, held in the back of their throat, like this: 'Hullo'. Because in Glasgow it's always raining, you see, so everybody has their heads down.

The Man Play it again.

Anna rewinds and plays the tape again.

I don't know. What do you think?

Anna I suppose it sounds soft. Like you said.
Softly spoken.
Maybe you come from a soft landscape?

The Man Somewhere with rolling hills. Low hills.

Anna Yes.

The Man And farmland. Copses.

Anna Does that landscape ring any bells?

The Man It certainly feels familiar.

Anna Of course it may not mean anything. I'm not really here to investigate that per se. Really I just need to establish that you're British and see if I can set out a process for the investigation. Hopefully just by talking we can establish a few background details. Then we'll send the tape to a forensic specialist in the UK who can analyse the tape.
Come up with something more specific.
And eventually we'll try to match what we've got against the missing-persons records.

The Man I do seem to feel an affinity with nature.
I've been appreciating the arrival of spring.
Seeing the birds come back.
Just these past few days.

Anna It's gorgeous, isn't it?
Not like Britain.

14

The Man Things coming to life again.

Anna You feel it, don't you? One does.

The Man Very strongly.
  You were an actress?

Anna Yes. Well, you know, a long time ago.

The Man Can't have been that long ago.

Anna I gave it up. It wasn't really me.

The Man That's a shame.

Anna Well, it's not so much that I wasn't any good. I was
– well – that's for others to judge. I just don't think I was
cut out for it.

The Man Learning all those lines.

Anna No. I could learn the lines. I think it was more that
I didn't seem to fit a 'type'.

  The Man is staring at Anna.

In theatre people often cast by 'type'. And I – didn't seem
to have one – well, I don't know – my face didn't fit.
Whatever it was. Maybe it was that I'm – you know, my
weight.

The Man . . .

Anna Anyway, lah-di-dah.
  It doesn't matter.
  Is everything all right?

The Man Hm?

Anna It's just you were . . .

The Man I was looking at you. Sorry.

Anna It's all right.
  I don't mind you looking.

15

I was just worried for a moment.
That you were ill.

The Man Sometimes I get a feeling when I'm speaking to a person.
Like an undertow.

Anna Oh.
Perhaps that's important.
An undertow?

The Man I can't really describe it in more detail than that, I'm afraid.
But I have that feeling with you.

Anna Is it a feeling of recognition?

The Man I don't know.

Anna Of course, if you felt you recognised me, that would be odd.
I mean, I know you've never met me before.
Because I would remember.

The Man You're right.

Anna But maybe I remind you of someone?

The Man No. It isn't that.
It's gone.
I'm not sure I could have put a word to it anyway.

Anna OK.
Never mind.

The Man Sorry.

Anna God, there's no need to apologise.
I wasn't –
This must be very difficult for you.

The Man It's embarrassing.

Anna Please don't be embarrassed.

The Man No, I mean, not knowing who I am.

It isn't difficult really except when . . . well, in social situations, it's embarrassing.

Anna Please don't be embarrassed with me.

I'm here to help. You're not under suspicion or in any kind of trouble. Far from it.

A lot of people have an idea about consular staff that we're stuck up, or cold, out to get them. But we're not.

I think we're like doctors.

We just try to sort out people's problems.

The Man Have you ever had anyone like me before?

Anna I believe it's happened, not in France but somewhere.

I once heard about it.

It isn't common, no. But that's the thing about consular work – every day is different.

The Man Today you're a detective.

Anna Not really a detective.

The Man A puzzler.

Anna It's certainly one of the more interesting cases I've had.

The Man If it's any help.

I'm pretty sure I'm British.

Anna We can't be sure of anything.

The Man You're right but, you know, just then – when you were talking about the consular staff. Suddenly I felt proud. It was a feeling of pride in the British Diplomatic Service.

Why would I feel proud of the British Diplomatic Service?

Unless I was British?

Anna I'll just take a note of that. (*Anna takes a note of that.*) Maybe we should begin with – if you're comfortable, if you could just – for the tape, to get an example of your speech down, if you could just – I don't know – describe where we are, what you can see?

The Man Um.
    We're on the terrace. A terrace.
    Around us there are tables and chairs.
    Below us there's a steep slope, a mountain pasture,
    Stretching away down.
    Over there – there's a sheer rock face.
    It's very rugged.
    Beautiful.
    Very typical of the Pyrenees, I suppose.
    Is that enough?

Anna Perhaps a little bit more.
    It's not so much what you see as the words you use to
    describe it that are important.

The Man ...

Anna Just keep going.
    Try to be natural.

The Man The sky is blue. Porcelain-blue.
    White cirrus clouds high up.
    Evangeline's hanging up laundry.
    She's talking to one of the climbers.
    She's laughing.
    I can see the climbers' tents further up in the pasture.
    ...
    A pine forest behind us.
    The smell of a thaw.
    ...
    Look, as a matter of fact, describing things feels
unnatural.

Anna It's good. Keep going.

The Man A . . . through the pines . . . a river, not a river but a . . .
There's a word for it.
Smaller than a river –

Anna Stream?

The Man Stream. Yes. I suppose. Running through the pines.

Anna It wasn't the word you were looking for?

The Man No.
'Buh . . . ' 'Buh . . . '
It's on the tip of my tongue.

Anna Brook?

The Man No.

Anna Beck?

The Man No.

Something of a pause.

It's gone.

Anna If it had been 'beck' then we could have said that you were from Yorkshire, you see, or at least the north of England, or at least that you have some connection with the north.

The Man Right. I get you. The words are a clue.
I'm sorry I can't –
'Buh . . . '
No.

Anna We'll tape some more later.
There's no rush.
I'm just here to get to know you and write down whatever I think might help the experts.
I think we should try to be relaxed about it.

No point rushing.
Just . . .
Take it as it comes.

The Man I might be from Yorkshire.
York.
No.
Nothing stirring.
York.

Anna While you think about that, I'll just write some of this down.
Do you mind if I smoke?

The Man Not at all.

Anna takes out a cigarette and lights it.
She writes on her pad.
Something of a pause.

There's something about the smoke.
The smell.

Anna I am sorry. Is it blowing in your face?

The Man It's familiar.
Do you – do you mind? Could I have a cigarette?

Anna I'm sorry. I didn't offer. I just assumed you didn't smoke.

The Man I haven't. Not since I've been here.
But the smell is definitely familiar.
I'm just wondering if it's familiar because I'm a smoker.
Do you see?

Anna The smell of smoke would be familiar to someone who lived with a smoker. Just because it's familiar doesn't mean that you're a smoker.

The Man I won't know unless I try it, will I?

Anna Yes, but that's something you wouldn't want to find out.
　You don't want to discover that you're a smoker.
　Not if you've given up.

The Man No. I'm pretty sure I am a smoker.

Anna People go to endless lengths to give up smoking.
　I know – believe me – I'm weak myself.
　So even if you were a smoker – you've given up so –

The Man Just give me a fag.

Anna . . .

Anna offers him the packet.
He takes a cigarette.
He lights it.

The Man Yes. This feels very familiar. This feels . . . yes . . .
　Like coming home.

Anna I'm sorry.
　I shouldn't have been smoking myself.
　Not when I'm working.

The Man Don't worry about it.

Anna Now I've got you started.

The Man You didn't offer me heroin, Miss Edwards.

Anna I know.

The Man We're making progress.

Anna Anna.

The Man I know.

Anna Sorry.

The Man I'm a smoker.

I'm not from Yorkshire.
It's not much, but it's a start.

Anna This must be terribly difficult for you.

The Man It's fine.
I have money. A place to stay. My health.
I'm happy.
There are people much worse off than me.
It's kind of you to be concerned but –
I don't think I like fuss.
I think I'm the kind of person who doesn't like a fuss being made of them.

Anna I know what you mean.
I'm like that myself.

The Man Are you?

Anna I like to be left alone.

The Man Not completely alone.

Anna Can't get into trouble on my own.

The Man Not fussed over.

Anna No.

The Man That's it.
That's what I'm like.

Anna I respect that.

The Man Thank you.

Anna Do you mind if I ask, as much for my own curiosity as anything else: what do you remember? –
I mean – do you have any memories?

The Man I remember being found in the snow.
I remember everything since then.

Anna But before? I mean, how do you know where you are?

The Man Well, I'm here.

Anna No – but where is here?

The Man The terrace.

Anna Yes but –

The Man The Pyrenees.
France.

Anna And France – what is France?

The Man I'm not clear what you mean?

Anna Does France mean anything to you?

The Man France is a country.

Anna Do you know what a country is?

The Man Yes.

Anna I see.
. . .
What's the capital of Uruguay?

The Man Montevideo.
Look, I can see what you're getting at. Clearly I still have whatever bank of general knowledge I built up in my previous . . . existence. But when I bring that knowledge to mind, what's missing is my place in it. I'm absent. I have no idea how I came to know it. Do you see?

Anna Your accent has a lilt.
You became quite animated just then and I noticed a slight lilt to your accent.

The Man A lilt?
Maybe it does.
Can you place it?

23

Anna No . . . Wales? . . . '*know* it', 'no idea how I came
to *know* it'.
  Wales?
  '*Know* it'.
  The experts will get it.
  We should tape you when you're animated.
  Hold on.

She picks up the tape recorder again.
  Prepares to press record.

You're looking at me again.

The Man I know.
  It's an undertow of warmth.
  I'm getting it again.

Anna Warmth.
  That's interesting.
  Particularly when I just mentioned Wales.

The Man Miss Edwards. Anna.
  This is a little embarrassing.
  . . .
  I seem to want to hold you.

Anna I see.

The Man It's going.
  The feeling's fading.

Anna Get it back, try – describe it.

The Man Wanting to hold you.
  And a feeling of wanting to tell you about the feeling.

Anna Hold me.

The Man Are you sure?

Anna It's quite all right.

The Man leaves his chair. He goes over to Anna's chair.
  Anna stands up.
  He holds her. He remains that way for some moments.
  He breaks off.

He returns to his chair.
  He sits down.

Anna Gosh.

The Man I'm sorry.

Anna sits down again.

Anna No. It's good. It's –

The Man I can't help it. I just had the feeling –

Anna Actually, because I used to be an actress, and
also because I've worked so long in a Mediterranean
country, I'm actually more comfortable with that sort of
spontaneous physical contact than most people. It's really
– it's OK.

The Man I feel embarrassed now.

Anna Don't.

The Man I'm sweating.
  God.
  I'm really sorry.
  You're here to do a job, not to have me pawing over
you like some Norwegian pig.

Anna It's OK.
  It's OK.
  Norwegian?

The Man What?

Anna You said, 'like some Norwegian pig'.

The Man Yes.

Anna Why Norwegian?

The Man It's just, 'Norwegian pig', a figure of speech.
Just –
. . .
Isn't it?
'Norwegian pig'. Surely that's a phrase, isn't it?

Anna I've never heard it before.

The Man Disgusting pig. Pig anyway. It doesn't matter.

Anna You held me.
It wasn't disgusting.

Something of a pause.

The Man In the snow, the feeling I had when I opened
my eyes.
I had a feeling of extraordinary –
I can't put a word to it.
Cleanliness.
A feeling of whiteness, of cold, but also a feeling of
The most enormous relief.
As though I'd woken up screaming from a dream I
couldn't remember.
Sometimes, when you ask questions, I feel as though
I'm going to fall somewhere. In my head.

Anna I understand.

The Man If I've forgotten, maybe I had good reason to
forget.

Anna I don't believe, if this is what you're saying, that
you're –
I'm no expert, but if it's any comfort, the impression
you give me is kindly. You seem kindly.

The Man What does that mean?

Anna A kindly soul. I'm known as being quite a good judge of character. I often wonder if I'm not slightly psychic actually.

I once met Slobodan Milosovic at a reception and I got an intense feeling of evil from him. As physical as if he was radiating heat. From you I get kindliness. Warmth. Strength.

The Man . . .

Anna We'll get to the bottom of it.

Anna holds his hand across the table.

What's your name?

The Man . . .

Anna . . .

Anna withdraws her hand.

The Man Why did you ask me that?
You know I don't know.
Were you trying to trick me?

Anna No.

The Man You don't believe me.

Anna Of course I do, I'm sorry, I –

The Man I don't know what my name is.
I don't know who I am.
How could I know what my name is?

Anna I thought, for a second, that you might answer from instinct.

The Man Don't you think I haven't tried that?

Anna It was silly of me.

The Man It's fine.

27

I'm sorry.
You didn't mean anything.

Anna No. It was clumsy. I overstepped the mark.

The Man I overreacted.
I think you touched a nerve.

Anna That might be significant, you know.

The Man Maybe.

Anna Sorry.

The Man Look, do you mind if we break for a bit?

Anna No. It's OK. It's a good idea. We'll take a break.

The Man My head's –

*He makes a gesture with his hands, suggesting his
thoughts are in a jumble.*

Anna Of course.

*The Man retreats to the edge of the terrace.
    Something of a pause.
    The Man returns.*

The Man Do you mind if I borrow a cigarette?
I'll buy some.

Anna Not at all.

The Man Thank you.

She offers a cigarette. He takes it and lights it.

I just need a moment to recover.

Anna Of course.

*The Man retreats again.
    He smokes.
    He looks at the view.*

The Proprietor enters.

The Proprietor Good morning, Miss Edwards.

Anna Morning.

The Proprietor Spring-like.

Anna Isn't it just?

The Proprietor And it's quiet. You can enjoy the peace.

Anna Yes.

The Proprietor The season hasn't really begun yet. This is the first time I've put tables out on the terrace. At the moment there's just you, the gentleman and the lady in room one hundred and eight. There are some climbers about but they camp on the pasture. They don't spend any money here. They'll be on the mountain soon. You can watch them. People watch them from the terrace with binoculars. Every year one or two of them falls. They want to climb. We want to watch. Some of them are bound to fall. What can I do?

I prepared a room for you. Room one hundred and nine. Whenever you're ready I'll take your bag up for you.

Anna Thank you. I think I'll be all right.

The Proprietor Whatever you prefer.
How is he?

Anna Oh, you know. It's . . .
It must be terribly difficult for him.

The Proprietor Obviously since he arrived I've been expecting a visit from someone, although you could have called ahead and I'd have prepared things for you. Yesterday, the gendarme, Bernard-Marie, told me to expect someone at some point, he wasn't any clearer than that – but then Bernard-Marie is not noted for his clarity.

I hope there isn't a problem. Is the gentleman in trouble? He's been very quiet. He comes down from his room every morning and sits on the terrace. He looks at the mountain. Bernard-Marie comes by in the afternoon to check he's still here. He talks to him. Bernard-Marie is struggling with inner demons, don't tell him I told you that, and I think he likes to talk things through with an Englishman. I don't count. If you ask me the man's a pilgrim. When they found him he was clutching a scallop shell. In all likelihood he's a pilgrim who's had a nervous breakdown, got lost in the snow, and . . . now here he is.

I play chess with him. He's a poor chess player, but no one else here plays at all so . . . He pays for the room by the day. He doesn't complain. I'll be sad to see him go. Do you have an idea who he is? I don't want to know. If he's done something awful, I don't want to know.

Anna What makes you think he's done something awful?

The Proprietor How old do you think he is?

Anna I don't know, late fifties . . . ?

The Proprietor Do you know any man, or any person for that matter, but let's be more specific, do you know any man, any man at all who has reached the age of fifty without at any stage in his life having done something awful. Some awful act, or failure to act, which he regrets bitterly. Some act which would come back to him nightly and bring beads of sweat to his forehead. Some act which he would yearn to erase.

Anna Well, I don't know . . .

The Proprietor Take it from me.

Anna But people . . . sometimes people are ashamed of perfectly reasonable things. Maybe he wanted to erase something that happened to him. Something he was a victim of.

The Proprietor Perhaps. I hope you're right.

Anna And people are capable of good.

The Proprietor Sporadically.

Anna So, you know, he's just as likely to have done good things, to be a good person, a person whom someone loves. Someone who someone else needed, needs even.

The Proprietor What are the chances?

Anna Do you speak to him about this?

The Proprietor No. Of course not.
  I play chess with him. That's all. Really. He's been the perfect gentleman. Can I bring you a pot of coffee?

Anna Thank you.

The Proprietor Shall I ask him if he wants anything?

Anna Leave him just now.

The Proprietor Do you have inside information?
  You must have an idea.
  The British police must have an idea.
  Has he done something awful?
  No I actually don't want to know.

Anna Really I'm only here to establish if he's our responsibility.
  Once I've done that I'll be out of your hair.

The Proprietor Oh, he's definitely British.
  I'll go further than that. He's English. I'd put my shirt on it.
  I haven't lived in England since I was a tiny boy.
  Who'd want to?
  Really.
  I occasionally go to London on business.
  Dearie me.

But I can tell an Englishman when I see one.
We still carry a certain bearing.
Wouldn't you say?

Anna I don't know. I'm not an expert. I'm just . . . I'm really just a . . . it's quite an unusual job for me, in fact. It's not part of my regular duties.

The Proprietor Suggestion.
Ask him if he likes to spank or be spanked.
I've never known an Englishman who doesn't like one or the other.
For a Spaniard, like me, to have sex is to enter into a zone of ritualised combat between oneself and death.
The German in me thinks of sex like eating – a gustatory business, all fingers, juices and smells.
My Italian side requires an audience and applause.
The Portugese in me simply wants to weep at the sadness of beauty.
Ah well.
Do you like to spank or be spanked?

Anna . . .

The Proprietor You're embarrassed. It's well seen you're English.

Anna Actually I'm not. As it happens I'm Welsh.

The Proprietor Fiery.
Don't mind me. I flirt with all the clientele.
It's the Frenchman in me.
You musn't take me seriously.

Anna Right.

The Proprietor It's been a long winter.
I've barely talked to anyone since last November.
. . .
I'll get your coffee.

He's looking over here.
Morning.

The Man Morning.

The Proprietor Well. Good luck.
I don't want to know.
I take as I find.

The Proprietor exits.
He returns with a tray and a coffee.
He puts it down in front of her.

Will there be anything else?

Anna No. I'm fine. Thank you. This is fine. Thank you.

The Proprietor remains for a moment.
Anna takes out her purse.
She takes out some money, offers it to him.

Thank you.

The Proprietor It's not necessary to offer me a gratuity.
I am the proprietor, madam.

Anna Oh, I'm so sorry.

The Proprietor If there's nothing else.

Anna No. No. I'm fine. I'm sorry.

The Proprietor It's not necessary to be sorry for offering
me a gratuity, madam.

Anna Right.
Silly.

The Proprietor exits.
The Man comes back over to Anna and sits down.

The Man I've been thinking.
I'm wondering if I might be from Bristol.

Or at least the West Country.
Cheltenham, or Swindon, or Gloucester.

Anna Right.

The Man It's the landscape. It's . . . soft, and I do seem
to have a sense of low hills, woodland and mists . . .
which is –

Anna You don't have a strong accent.

The Man That doesn't necessarily mean anything.
I may have lost the accent.
Or else I may be – you see I have money – maybe I'm
middle-class.
Perhaps I'm a person from the West Country but with
a standard accent.
R.P.
Neutral.

Anna I suppose it's worth following up.

The Man There's something else as well.
As I was standing there, smoking, and by the way I'm
convinced now that I am a smoker, I saw a woman
walking on the pasture. The woman from room one
hundred and eight. She was walking down the path
towards the . . . what's that word – stream. And I had a
feeling . . .

Anna The undertow.

The Man That's right. And I thought to myself, 'There
she is, walking the downs.' The word 'downs' came to
me. From nowhere.
But that's a West Country word, isn't it?

Anna You might be right.

The Man It might be nothing.

. . .

I just started to get a picture of myself.

34

As a boy, amongst a soft landscape.
And growing up, and needing to leave.
A sense of myself as a sailor, of some kind.
Of the pull of the sea.
And a feeling that life held more for me.
Adventure.
Dolphins – a picture of dolphins amongst the foam at
the prow of a fast-moving boat.
The company of men.
It's all very vague, but . . .
What do you think.

Anna I'm sorry?

The Man You seem distracted.

Anna Oh. Yes.
I think I just offended the proprietor.

The Man Pedro?

Anna Is that his name?

The Man One of them.

Anna He was hovering.
I offered him a tip.

The Man Oh no.

Anna I know. I didn't realise.

The Man It's fine.
Pedro's –
He'll understand.

Anna Maybe I should go and apologise.

The Man Pedro's fine.

Anna I'm Welsh but I'm so bloody English.
Ugh.
I often think. I often think India would never have
been part of the British Empire if, when the first ship

came, the Indians had stood on the shoreline looking as if they might or might not require a tip. I think the English would have frozen. I think they would have run away.

The Man I never tip. On principle. I'm a socialist.
Born and bred.

Anna Really?

The Man I don't know where that came from.

Anna What?

The Man I wonder if it's true.

Anna About tipping?

The Man About me – being a socialist – what I said.
I don't know where it came from.
But the words felt familiar as I said them.

Anna Maybe things are starting to come back to you?

The Man Maybe.
. . .
Why would a socialist be against tipping?

Anna When I was a waitress, I hated non-tippers.

The Man You would.
It seems perverse.

Anna It's downright inconsiderate.

The Man I must have been a git.

Anna Mean.

The Man A Jock.

Anna laughs.

Anna I shouldn't laugh.

The Man laughs.

The Man A mean-spirited, depressed, dour, violent, Jock.
Making everybody miserable.

. . .

No wonder I went mad.

They both laugh.

Anna I was just thinking – about the breakfast – you
mentioned you had the full English?

The Man You're worried about my health again.

Anna Well – yes – smoking, cholesterol . . .
No, it's just I wondered – the full English breakfast.
I wondered.
Is that what you've had every morning.

The Man Since I've been here.

Anna I just wonder if that – might mean you're English.
If you see what I mean.

The Man I do.

Anna You're a man who eats a full English breakfast.
That's your preference.

The Man Although I always dither over the continental.

Anna Maybe in your previous – maybe – before – maybe –

The Man Maybe.
But then – what if I was the sort of man who ate a
continental breakfast out of concern for my health but
deep down had always wanted to eat a full English? That
would explain the dithering.

Anna You're right.
It's probably nothing.

The Man For example.
I've shown a marked preference for coffee.
Even though they offer tea here.

But that's not very English, is it?
To drink coffee?

Anna Well, these days . . . I don't know. I drink coffee
myself and I'm English. Well, as I say, Welsh.

The Man Welsh.

Anna Yes.

The Man If you hadn't said, I'd never have guessed.

Anna People don't.

The Man Where from in Wales?

Anna You wouldn't know it.

The Man I suppose not.

Anna To be honest, I say I'm Welsh, my father came
from Wales. I was actually brought up in Essex.
    So . . . whatever that means.
    And then I went to school in Yorkshire.
    Nuns.
    And then I went to university in Brighton.
    And then I joined the Diplomatic Service, so I've lived
in Tel Aviv and in Gaberone and now here I am in
France.
    But if pressed
    I think of myself as Welsh.
    Whatever that means.

Something of a pause.

Let's carry on.
    I mean, there isn't much more to do.
    I think we've established that you're English.
    Quite possibly from the West Country.
    Probably middle-class, professional.
    At some point you may have worked on the sea.
    We have some material on tape for the forensic experts

38

to study. I think it's a safe bet that you're the responsibility of the British Embassy.

The Man I can't argue with that.

Anna All I need to do now, really, is to establish some details about your arrival here. And then I have everything I need.

The Man Whatever you need.

Anna Now, the report from the gendarmerie –

The Man Bernard-Marie.

Anna Yes.
I received a copy of his report.
He says that you were found in the snow in one of the high passes near here on the pilgrims' way to Santiago de Compostela. Two climbers on their way down from the pass saw you slumped in the snow, apparently unconscious. They approached you, found you were alive, and carried you down to here.

The Man That's my memory of events as well.

Anna They say you were found wearing a suit, and a coat. The coat was labelled 'Abercrombie and Fitch', the suit was labelled with a Geneva tailor's mark. Does any of that mean anything to you?

The Man Not in the slightest.

Anna Me neither.
The climbers also say that close beside you was a briefcase and that when you were brought back here they opened the briefcase with your permission and they saw it was filled with money, in euros. There was no other documentation in the case.

The Man Yes, that's right.

Anna And finally we know that in your hand, when you were found, you were holding a scallop-shell medallion.

The Man That's correct.

Anna The doctor who examined you found nothing physically wrong with you except things that could be explained by prolonged exposure to the cold and injuries to your feet consistent with having walked a long distance in inappropriate footwear.
    You have a scar on the left side of your forehead.

The Man Yes.

Anna But the doctors say that's from a previous injury.

The Man Having rested, I have to say I feel fine.

Anna So that's all we know from the reports.
    What I wondered is if you could add to this stuff . . .

The Man Not really.

Anna What do you remember about the snow?

The Man I really remember the moment.
    Very intense.
    Of waking up – in the snow.
    That moment's where I start from. Now. New.
    A moment in the snow and being born, I suppose.

Anna This was when the climbers found you?

The Man Oh, before they found me.
    When I woke up.
    Amongst the snow.
    Something happened to me.

Anna Like waking up from a terrible dream?

The Man I saw – not saw, felt – experienced . . .
    I . . .
    I . . .
    Can't describe it.

Anna Was it . . . you must have been . . . you just woke up, amongst snow?

The Man Yes.

Anna With no memory of how you got there?

The Man None.

Anna Cold? Afraid?

The Man The opposite of afraid.
The opposite of cold.

Anna Warm? Safe?

The Man More. More than that. Something . . .

Anna Like – like what?

The Man Like having been scourged.

Anna Gee-whizz.

The Man Not being scourged – having been scourged. No memory of the scourging itself – only the raw afterwards –
Put your bare skin against snow for long enough.
That feeling.
Burning.

Anna And did you know that you'd forgotten who you were?

The Man No.
It was the opposite.
I had an intense understanding of exactly who I was.

Anna What do you mean?

The Man I was everything.
Everything was me.
There was no 'me'.

41

Anna One-ness?

The Man Doesn't capture it.

Anna Connection?

The Man No, more and . . .
No.

Anna A religious feeling? A sense of the presence of God?

The Man Maybe –

Anna Look.
I'm wondering. I may be way off beam here . . .
Do you have any history of epilepsy?

The Man How would I know?

Anna Of course. I forgot.
It's just – some of the symptoms.
In the immediate moments before a fit.
I've felt . . .
It's called an aura.
An enormous intensity of sensation.
With me it's smell.
Or, more accurately, a memory of a smell.
And then, coming round afterwards.
It's . . .
A sense one has been made aware of another world.
Is it like that?

The Man Do you mind if we . . .?
Can we . . .?
I feel quite tired.

Anna Of course. I'm sorry. We have plenty of time.

The Man I find it, all this, I suddenly find it terribly burdensome.
I'm sweating like a pig.

Anna It's warm.
  It's definitely warm.

The Man There was a scallop-shell medallion in my
pocket.
  Look.

  He takes out the scallop shell.

That means I'm a pilgrim.
  To be given shelter.

Anna The proprietor told me about it. I know.

The Man So obviously.
  Whoever I am – was. Was.
  Was on a pilgrimage.
  And whoever I was I – found –
  I had an experience.
  And –
  So . . . I don't really see what business the British
Embassy has – deciding who I am.
  I'm sorry, I was overtaken by a feeling.
  I'm sorry.

  Something of a pause.

Interrogating me.

  Something of a pause.

Implying that I'm mentally subnormal.

  Something of a pause.

It's not you.
  You're fine.
  It's the whole . . .

  *He makes a gesture with his hands suggesting that the
  world is jumbled up.*

Clanjamfrie.

43

Anna I'm sorry?

The Man Clanjamfrie.

Anna I don't understand.

The Man Jumble. Noise. Mess – you know.

Anna Clanjamfrie?

The Man Don't you know the word?

Anna No.

The Man It's like 'palaver'. Or . . . 'shenanigans'.

Anna Is it Welsh? It doesn't sound Welsh.

The Man It's an old word.
Everybody knows it. It's an old word people use with children.
Your mother comes into your bedroom and looks around and says –
'Goodness me, what a clanjamfrie.'

Anna Is it to do with Edward Lear?

The Man Look it up.
There must be a dictionary.
I don't know.
It may well be Old Cornish.
Given the West Country connection.

Anna It could be a clue.

The Man You keep picking up on words. It's just a word.
It doesn't mean anything.

Anna You said your mother used it.

The Man Did I?

Anna She would come into your room.

The Man I don't really remember.

44

Anna It's OK
  I've noted it.
  I'll look it up.
  It's probably nothing.

The Man I'm sorry for being difficult.

Anna It's all right.

The Man I seem to be quite a volatile person, don't I?
  Quite stormy.

Anna It's perfectly understandable in the circumstances.

The Man The world seems so beautiful.

Anna You nearly died.

The Man Quite volatile.

There is a catch in The Man's throat.
  He starts to cry in the manner of one for whom
crying is not at all easy.
  He may well not have cried for over thirty years.
  It's a sort of cracking.

Quite unlike myself.

Anna holds his hand again across the table.
  He manages to control the noise of his crying.
  But he still weeps.

I don't know why I'm crying.

He laughs.

Anna It's good.

The Man It's good.

Anna Let it out.

Very abruptly the crying has stopped.

Let it all out.

45

The Man Sorry about that.

Anna You just cry all you like.

The Man I'm fine now.
I don't know what came over me.

Anna Let it go.

> *Something of a pause.*
> *Anna seems to expect him to continue crying, but*
he doesn't.
> *They are still holding hands.*

The Man Look.
Is it possible we've met before?

Anna I don't think so.

The Man No.

Anna But I know what you mean.

The Man Do you?

Anna I think so.

The Man A sense.

Anna Yes.
Quite dim but –

The Man I feel more comfortable with you than seems . . .

Anna Exactly.

The Man You sense that.

Anna More comfortable, very suddenly comfortable.
Which one doesn't normally feel.

The Man No.

Anna Certainly not in these circumstances.

The Man A strong sense that I like you.
  I feel that.
  Quite strange.

Anna It isn't that strange because I have the same feeling.
  The same –

The Man I don't mean anything by it. I don't – but –

Anna You have – I think you have something – some –
I believe people are – that we're – somehow that we have
a –
  You know – a – something spiritual almost.

The Man I know it's silly.

Anna No, it isn't.

  Something of a pause.

It's getting dark.

The Man It gets dark quickly here.
  The sun goes behind the mountain.
  It gets chilly quite quickly.

Anna I booked a room for the night.
  So I'm . . .

The Man Right.

  The Proprietor enters.
    He is dressed in a formal black waiter's uniform.
    He puts candles in bottles on the tables and lights
  them.

The Proprietor Good evening, sir.
  Good evening, madam.

Both Good evening.

The Proprietor A beautiful evening.

47

Anna Yes.

The Proprietor We're very lucky.

Anna Yes. About before . . .

The Proprietor Madam?

Anna When I – I offered you a tip –

The Proprietor I don't remember, madam.

Anna Before.
When you came out here.

The Proprietor It must have been one of the other staff.

Anna No, it was you.

The Proprietor I'm the waiter, madam.
My shift only begins at six.

Anna It was you and – anyway I wanted to apologise . . .

The Proprietor Do you think we all look the same,
madam?
Wogs begin at Calais?
Is that it?
Is that what you're suggesting?

The Man Pedro.

Anna Of course not.

The Man Pedro's the waiter.

Anna Right.
Obviously I made a mistake.
I do apologise.

The Proprietor There's no need to apologise, madam.
A lot of English people make the same mistake.
I like to – you would call it – 'wind them up'.
Like a clockwork toy.

I was born in Africa. We Africans think it's fun to tease you bwanas.

I don't mean anything personal by it.

Anna I see.

The candle is on the table and lit.

The Proprietor Can I bring you something to drink? An aperitif?

Anna and The Man look at each other.

Anna Yes, please.

The Man Wine.

Anna A bottle of the house red.

The Man Thank you.

The Proprietor You're welcome.

The Proprietor leaves.

Anna Oh God.

The Man What?

Anna I've offended him again.

The Man You shouldn't have mentioned the tip.

Anna I wanted to apologise.

The Man It was forgotten.

When you offered to tip him, he saw you were embarrassed. Pedro wants to make everyone feel comfortable. He's a natural host.

And he decided to pretend the incident never happened.

He pretended to be someone else, so you would feel comfortable again.

But you mentioned it.

He couldn't back down – because that would have drawn attention to his motives and made you feel even more uncomfortable. So he turned it into a joke.
That's all.
It's best to leave it.

Anna God.
Why can't he just –

The Proprietor comes back in with the wine.
He uncorks the bottle.
Pours a little into Anna's glass.

Anna tastes it.

That's fine, thank you.

The Proprietor pours the wine into both glasses.
He places the bottle back on the table.

He stands a little back from the table, hovering.

Cheers.

The Man . . .

The Proprietor exits.

Anna What?

The Man He was expecting a tip.

Anna But –

The Man He thought that, given the fuss you've made about it, tipping made you feel comfortable.
He was waiting for a tip.

Anna Oh, for God's sake.

Anna laughs.

The Man Cheers.
. . .
It's nice to hear you laugh.

Anna I'm just – how ridiculous.

The Man You don't feel so bad now, do you?

Anna No.

The Man You don't feel awkward?

Anna He's the one with a stick up his arse. Not me.

The Man You're more relaxed.

Anna Yes.
Thank God.

The Man He's a tremendously good chess player.

Anna He's a character.

The Man Very interesting man.
Very interesting life.

Anna Like you.

Something of a pause.

The Man Do you mind if I say something which might seem
quite personal.

Anna No.
Sun's over the yardarm.
We're off work – aren't we?

The Man I think so.

Anna I think so too.

The Man So I can speak personally?

Anna Depends what it is.

The Man You strike me as quite a delicate person.
I don't mean you're not strong.
I just mean you're delicately balanced.

Anna Go on.

The Man And I think that when you say things like –
you have a weight problem. When obviously you don't.
You're quite slim. Or when you – you apologise for
yourself.
  I feel.
  You're uncomfortable with yourself.
  You don't like yourself.
  And that makes you unhappy.

Anna Gosh.
  Whoo.

The Man I'm sorry if I've offended you.

Anna No.
  God, you're right. No.

The Man You're aware of it?

Anna I'm aware of it – when am I not aware of it?

  . . .

  I'm just unnerved.
  A person saying it to me.

The Man Since my experience in the snow.
  I see some things more clearly.
  And I –
  For what it's worth.
  I sensed you wouldn't mind me saying it.

Anna Not at all.

  Something of a pause.

The Man There's something else.

Anna Hmm.

The Man Something I've noticed.

Anna Gosh.

Something else.

. . .

Mephisto.

The Man I think the undertow . . .
The sense
Between us.
I might be wrong.
But I think it's sexual.

Something of a pause.
Anna sips her wine.

The Man I know there's something unlikely about it.
I'm older than you.
And I'm not –
And you're –
But nonetheless, it's what I sense.

Anna I need more wine.

Some music starts to play from a speaker hung above
the terrace.
It isn't played loudly.
But after its absence it is momentarily intrusive.

The Man Pedro's tape.
He plays tapes in the evenings.

Anna pours more wine into her glass.
The music playing is 'Toto – Africa', Procul Harum.

I love this song.

Anna So do I.
I haven't heard this song for years.

The Man I wonder if I knew it before.

Anna There's something terribly poignant about this
song.
Something so sad.

The Man Perhaps there's a clue in it.

They listen to the song.
   For quite a period of time.
   They search for a clue.
   Anna takes his hand.
   The music continues.

Anna There is something . . .
Between us.
Isn't there?

Vivienne enters.
   The music stops.
   Vivienne is dressed for walking in the hills.
   She is wearing heavy boots.
   She stops.

Vivienne Evening.

Both Evening.

Vivienne clomps across to a nearby table.
   She sits.
   She starts taking her boots off.

Vivienne Lovely evening.

Anna Isn't it just?

Vivienne It was hot earlier on.

Anna Yes.
Where were you walking?

Vivienne Oh, up through the forest.
I was following the pilgrims' way.

Anna Lovely.

Vivienne (*introducing herself*) Vivienne Sutherland.

Anna Anna Edwards.
I work for the British Consulate in Marseilles.

The Man has stood up to shake Vivienne's hand.

The Man Nice to meet you, Vivienne.

A slightly awkward moment.

Anna This is Bob – Abercrombie.
A friend of mine.

Vivienne Bob.

They shake hands.
Vivienne sits back down and continues to take her boots off.

It's absolutely beautiful in the pine forest.
It took me the whole morning walking before I reached the snow.
I saw a deer.
Drinking at the burn.
Caught in the sunlight.
Just idyllic.

Anna It sounds lovely.
Would you like to join us?

Vivienne Are you sure?

Anna We were just – we're – we were – We're only having a drink.
Please.

Vivienne I've been walking all day.
I'll just go up to my room.
Wash the dust off.

Anna Lovely.

Vivienne leaves.

I felt I had to invite her.

The Man It's all right.

55

Anna I didn't mean to spoil our . . . whatever.

The Man Of course.

Anna I was just being polite.

The Man Look.
I – what I said before.
It's best if we forget it.

Anna Why?

The Man You're younger than me and –
I'm sorry.
I got a bit 'spazzy'.

Anna laughs.

I should have kept my big mouth shut.

Anna No.

The Man Stupid. Stupid. Oh God.

Anna Please don't be like this.

The Man I feel sick.

Anna Please.

The Man I'm actually going to have to be sick.
I'm sweating like a pig.

Anna I wish I knew your name.

The Man Why?

Anna I want to say it to you.
I want to say your name to soothe you.

The Man I'll tell you one thing.
It isn't fucking Bob.
Bob fucking Abercrombie.
Sort of fucking name is that?

The Man leaves.

Excuse me.

> *The Proprietor enters with another glass.*
> *He puts the glass on the table.*

The Proprietor Can you still see in the dark?
Out here in the dark?
Would you like some coloured lights?

> *He switches on some coloured lights.*

Is that better?

Anna That's fine.

> *He tries a different combination.*

The Proprietor That any good?

Anna Fine, thank you.

> *He tries another.*

The Proprietor How about that?

Anna Fine. Fine it's –

The Proprietor Just trying to catch a mood.

> *He tries another combination.*

That do you?

Anna That's fine. Only I get headaches if lights go on
and off –

The Proprietor Everything has to be just so. Fussy.
Pernickety. Is that it?

Anna Sorry.

The Proprietor Typical woman.

Anna I'm sorry.

The Proprietor I was talking about me.

Vivienne enters.

Vivienne Evening, Pedro, what a lovely night. Haven't you done a good job with those lights?

The Proprietor The snow's melting, the forest's full of water, the earth is unbinding itself – who knows what spirits are abroad, Mrs Sutherland?
The lights confuse them, keeps them hiding in the dark. All part of the package.

Vivienne notices the empty chair.

Vivienne Where's . . . Bob?

Anna He wasn't feeling very well.

Vivienne Oh dear, that's a pity.

Anna Probably something he ate.

Vivienne Poor man.

Anna Mm.

Vivienne indicates the third chair.

Vivienne May I –

Anna Of course.

Vivienne sits.
Silence.

The Proprietor remains, hovering.

Look, do you mind?
He said he was feeling sick.
I think I'll just go up to his room.
Check that he's all right.

Vivienne D'you know, Anna,
I don't think that's such a good idea.

Anna I'm sorry?

Vivienne I think we should leave him for now.

Anna I'm not clear what you're getting at.

Vivienne Perhaps you should have a look at this.

Vivienne puts a photograph on the table.
She opens it.
Anna looks at it.

Anna Is this . . . This is –

Vivienne Yes. It is.
I don't know what he's told you about himself, Miss Edwards, but I know who he is. I know him.
Oh, by the way, Pedro. The hairdryer socket in my room isn't working.
Would you see to it for me, please?

End of Act One.

Act Two

The next morning.
  Vivienne is sitting on the terrace.
  The Man enters.
  Something of a pause.

The Man Apparently you're my wife.

Vivienne Keith.

The Man Keith.

  . . .

  Keith.

Vivienne Keith Sutherland.

The Man Pedro said you had a photograph.

Vivienne Sit down.

  Something of a pause.
    The Man sits down.
    Vivienne pushes the photograph to him.
    He looks at the photograph.
    After a time:

It was taken at the Fisheries Department ball.
  At the North British. Four Christmases ago.
  With the McColls.
  D'you remember?
  We went with the McColls.

The Man . . .

Vivienne That's Gavin, that's Trish, and that's you.
  We were all a bit tipsy.
  Your cheeks are red.

The Man This is Keith?

Vivienne That's you. That's right.

The Man This man. There's a superficial resemblance
but I don't think –

Vivienne It's you.

The Man I'm sorry, Mrs Sutherland.
I really have no memory of this event.
Of you.
Of any of this.

Vivienne Keith.
I know this can't be easy for you.
I didn't want to have to just come out with it.
That's why I waited.
I booked in to the hotel and I thought, I won't
introduce myself.
I'll just wait till he's ready.

The Man You've been watching me?

Vivienne I was waiting for you to come to yourself in
your own time.
I knew it wouldn't be easy for you.
And I wanted to be there when it happened.
To help you through.

The Man Don't you think that's a bit –

Vivienne But when I saw the woman from the Embassy.
I thought –

The Man I think this is a little bit sinister.

Vivienne I thought I ought to – because she was –

The Man Stalking me.

Vivienne She was clearly forming a bond.

The Man Which is none of your business.

Vivienne I am your wife.

The Man So you say.

Something of a pause.

You and your husband –

Vivienne Keith.

The Man Have you been married long?

Vivienne Twenty-eight years.

The Man Really.

Vivienne Twenty-nine in June.

The Man Right.

A pause.

Any children?

Vivienne No.

The Man Where is it that you said you live?

Vivienne In Edinburgh.

The Man I don't know Edinburgh.
It's supposed to be very nice.

Vivienne It's home.

The Man Your husband, is he a – what is he?

Vivienne A civil servant.
In the Fisheries Department.

The Man Really. How interesting.

. . .

Is he 'Edinburghian'?

Vivienne From Aberdeenshire originally.

The Man Fascinating.

Vivienne Near Aberdeen. A little place called Fyvie.

The Man Och aye the noo.
It's a braw bricht moonlicht nicht the nicht.

Vivienne Don't mock, Keith.

The Man I'm sorry.

> *Something of a pause.*
> *The Man looks at the photograph.*
> *The Man takes out a cigarette, lights it, smokes.*

Vivienne You've started smoking again.

The Man Was Keith a smoker?

Vivienne Keith had given up.

The Man Look, do you mind if I ask you a personal question?
You and Keith.
Were you – happily married?

Vivienne We were married. It wasn't unhappy.
We are –
Happy is probably not the most appropriate word, given the circumstances.

The Man I mean – whoever this Keith is –
He's run away, hasn't he?
He's run off.
Disappeared off the face of the earth.
So, you can see what I'm saying.
He can't have been –

Vivienne I think you were unhappy.
I think you'd probably been unhappy for some time.
I didn't know anything about it – everything seemed normal right up until the day you disappeared.

But it seems that normal for me was unhappy for you.
You were having an affair with a young woman in
London.
After a time you broke it off.
And you faked your own death.
You made it appear that you had walked into the sea.
. . .
That was quite hard for me.

The Man It must have been.

Vivienne We never talked, Keith.
We sat in that room night after night.
We sat quietly.
And we never talked.

The Man Really.

Vivienne If we'd only – if I'd only read the signs, but –
One falls into a rut, doesn't one?
And . . .
Certain things get left unsaid.

The Man Like what?

Vivienne Things.
Affectionate things.

The Man Affectionate things get left unsaid?

Vivienne I think they do. Sometimes.

The Man You've come here and I . . . Superficially I . . .
Is it it all possible that you're . . .

He makes a gesture of searching.

Do you think it's fair to say that you could be
Clutching at straws?

Vivienne You're still my husband, Keith.

The Man Really?

Vivienne Despite everything.

The Man Well that's . . .
  An admirable sentiment.

  Something of a pause.

Vivienne We've both changed.
  We're not the same people.
  I think –
  I know we can . . .
  I think it's worth trying at least.
  I'm not putting any pressure on you to come back.
  But for what it's worth.
  I've forgiven you.

The Man Oh. Well. Right. Thanks. Thank you.
  I'm glad that I'm forgiven.
  Thank you for that.
  That's certainly a weight off my mind.

Vivienne This isn't easy for me either.

The Man You see what I'm thinking is – this 'Keith'–
  Because I don't deny that you think I am Keith.
  And so – you know – it's only right that I take that
quite seriously –
  But you see – I look at you and –
  I think, well, is this a woman I could have . . . is it
possible that I was married to this woman? And then
I think –
  I apologise for being so blunt.
  I don't find you attractive.
  I'm not –
  . . .
  It's nothing personal.
  You're a very good-looking woman.
  You're just not my type.

Vivienne Keith, I'm old.

Your type, for the past couple of years,
Has been rather younger than me.
Girls who were playing you along.
Girls who didn't know any better.
Quite frankly, you made yourself look a little bit
pathetic.
I'm not being personal, Keith.
Many men make fools of themselves at your age.
You're no different.

The Man Even if I was Keith, and I'm not.
But even if I was.
It sounds from what you say that Keith's having quite
a nice time on his own, thank you very much.
Money, girls.
It sounds to me like perhaps
You ought to take a hint.

Vivienne takes another photograph from her pocket.
She puts it on the table.
The Man looks at it.

Who's this?

Vivienne This is just before we were married.
In the country, near your mum and dad's house.

The Man This is Keith again.
Good old Keithy.

Vivienne That's you. That's me. That's your mum and dad.

The Man laughs.

What?

The Man That beard.

Vivienne I liked your beard.

The Man I would never have a beard like that.

Something of a pause.

66

The landscape in the picture.
  That's where Keith is from?

Vivienne That's where you were brought up.

The Man That's not Scotland.
  Scotland has mountains.

Vivienne Not in the Howe of the Mearns.
  It's a farming area. Rolling hills, no mountains.
  Your dad was a teacher in the high school.
  He died about ten years ago.
  Your mum went just after.
  They were proud of you, Keith.

  A pause.

This is us on a walking holiday,
  With the University Labour Club.
  This is somewhere near Glastonbury, I think.
  I must be about twenty.
  That's where we met. One day you just started walking
with me.
  We walked together.

The Man You're very beautiful.

Vivienne Aren't I?

  A pause.

The Man I'm terribly sorry, Mrs Sutherland.
  I don't –
  I've listened to what you have to say and –
  Thank you for being so –
  But –
  No.
  No, this is not –
  I'm afraid I just –
  I do hope I haven't been a disappointment.

Vivienne I'm not in a hurry, Keith.
  I'm not going anywhere.
  Keep the pictures.
  I wanted to go for a walk before lunch anyway.
  You know where I am.

  Vivienne stands up.
    She prepares to leave.
    Anna enters.

Anna Don't mind me.
  If you're –

The Man Anna, good morning. I hope you slept well.

Anna I didn't want to interrupt.

The Man You're not interrupting anything.

Anna Do you mind if I join you?

Vivienne I was just going for a walk.

Anna It's a lovely morning.

Vivienne Isn't it.

Anna Look, if I'm in the way –

Vivienne No.
  You must have some – administration to do.
  I'll leave you to it.

  Vivienne leaves.
    Anna hesitates.
    Anna sits.
    She looks at the photographs.

Anna How do you feel?

The Man Oh, you know.

Anna It's a lot to take in.

The Man I'm not her husband.

. . .

Look,

Any woman could turn up here –

Could get wind of my situation and just turn up out of the blue.

And lay claim.

You know.

Just blah blah blah – there you go – that's it.

It's a good deal more complicated than that, don't you think?

Anna Of course.

The Man She was persuasive, I'll give her that.

Anna Well, the photograph does look like you –

The Man It looks like me. Looks like. Like.

But –

It's hardly evidence.

Anna Well . . .

The Man I was sitting there. Trying to be reasonable.

And she was talking about this man.

And how he ran away.

And what a bastard he was.

And I was feeling, you know, this tug of guilt.

You know.

Gnawing away.

Horrible taste in my mouth.

And oh – just – awful.

And then I thought,

How dare you?

After everything I've been through.

How dare you make me feel –

Exploit my situation for your own neurotic –

To satisfy your own sad fantasies.

Anna She is odd.

The Man Odd? She's – she's . . .
Certainly odd.

Anna And this business of staying here.
Having been here all this time and –

The Man It's pretty suspicious, isn't it?
Quite a lot of time to concoct . . .

Anna Yes.
. . .
Poor you.

The Man No. Honestly, I'm fine.

Anna What did she say your name was?

The Man Keith.

Anna laughs.

Anna Keith.
It is a bit ridiculous.

The Man laughs.
Something of a pause.

The Man About last night. I'm sorry.

Anna It's all right.

The Man No I . . . I was . . . I behaved quite badly.

Anna You were upset.

The Man I know, but –
I had no right to swear at you.

Anna I've heard worse.

The Man It wasn't right.

Anna I was worried about you.

I was about to follow you up to your room, to see if you were all right – and then she –

The Man She what?

Anna She showed me the picture.

The Man She showed you this?
    She had no right to –

Anna Yes. Well.
    And I . . . saw it and I thought –

The Man And you didn't come up to my room because she showed you the picture?

Anna Well. I suppose so.

Something of a pause.

The Man The bitch.

Anna I only wanted to see if you were all right.

The Man I was in my room.

Anna Because I knew you were upset.

The Man I was in my room and I –
    I have to be honest.
    I felt terrible about what I'd said to you.

Anna Honestly, I was fine about it.

The Man I hoped – I didn't think you would but I hoped –
    I watched BBC World.
    Lay on the bed with the remote.
    I actually didn't let myself fall asleep until after three because –
    I hoped you would come to my room.

Anna I was thinking about it.
    I was watching BBC World, thinking – should I . . .?

The Man I kept thinking, 'There'll be a knock.'

Anna I very nearly did.

The Man Of course there wasn't, and I –

Anna That ridiculous programme about Lech Walesa.
So annoying.

The Man Just absurd. Lech Walesa.

Anna And we were both lying there.

The Man And we could have been –

Anna So silly.

The Man I felt terrible about the way I'd spoken to you.

Anna You musn't.

The Man Because that isn't what I'm like.
I'm not – I don't want to be like that.

Anna You're not like that.

The Man But yesterday night. That woman's presence.
It was – baleful.
It upset me.

Anna The way you're coping with what's happened to
you.
It's brilliant. It's hardly surprising you get upset.

The Man I was waiting for you.

Anna I wanted to come.

Something of a pause.

The Proprietor enters.

The Proprietor Good morning, Miss Edwards.

Anna Good morning, Pedro.

The Proprietor Good morning, pilgrim.

The Man Good morning.

The Proprietor Can I bring you anything? A coffee? Aspirin?

The Man A coffee would be nice, thank you.

The Proprietor And for Miss Edwards?

Anna A coffee, thank you.

The Proprietor You look like you need one.

Anna laughs but not with pleasure.

The Welsh – there's no stopping a Welsh darkness, is there?

The Celtic twilight – I'm part Galician on my grandmother's side

I know about the Celtic twilight. The great black cloud that comes rolling in off the sea as darkness falls. 'The great fog' my grandmother called it. Sat on her chair looking out the window knocking back the brandy and weeping.

'Do not go gently into that good night.' Isn't that right? You Welsh – 'Rage rage against the dying of the light.'

Anna Ah, right. Dylan Thomas. Right.

The Proprietor I don't presume to pass comment, Miss Edwards.

We all self-medicate, don't we?

Some of us with chess.

Some of us with the minibar.

I'll get your coffee.

Strong.

The Proprietor exits.

Anna That was actually rude. He was rude to me.

The Man Pedro's OK.
He gets lonely up here, out of season.

Anna I'll have to interview the woman.

The Man It's an inconvenience for you. I'm sorry.

Anna Oh God. It's not your fault, it's hers.
I'll interview the woman.
I'll finish up my notes.
I'll take another sample of your speech,
And then I – have to go back to Marseilles.

The Man You have to leave today?

Anna I . . . well, unless – I don't like driving in the dark
so . . . if it all takes time then –

Something of a pause.

What you said last night.
About the undertow.

The Man Yes.

Anna I feel it too.
. . .
So yes, last night I got drunk – of course he has to
make something of it. He deliberately tried to upset me.
But last night after you went,
I felt very very alone.
And yes, I got drunk in my room.
Because I wanted to be with you.

The Man Anna.

He touches her hand.

Anna When I'm with you I catch a glimpse of a
possibility.
That I might be truly connected with someone.
And it's taken me by surprise.

74

Because I had stopped allowing myself to feel that possibility.
Just a few too many mistakes and one learns:
Shut that back in its box.
But you –
. . .
And last night I felt that witch was stealing it away from me.
I got drunk.
. . .
I was going to walk out of here this morning and forget the whole thing.

. . .
It's all right if you don't want any more to do with me.
Quite all right.
I understand perfectly.
I'm hardly a catch but –
. . .
I don't think possibilities come very often.
I had to say.

The Proprietor enters with coffees.
He puts them on the table.
He has a small pair of binoculars round his neck.

The Proprietor What a morning I'm having.
Evangeline's wailing like a baby in there.
She's supposed to be waitressing this shift.
But her boyfriend the climber told her this morning that he was going up the hill. To try a new route.
Evangeline's convinced he's going to die.
She dreamt it.
Honestly, I said to her – 'There are plenty more fish in the sea.
Do your work and put it out of your mind.'
But she refuses to come out on to the terrace.
She doesn't want to see him fall.

I said – keep your eyes on the customers.

But she's lying on the chaise longue clapping her hands and moaning like a bereaved seal.

I gave her the morning off.

The Man Poor Evangeline.

The Proprietor I brought you an aspirin and a glass of water anyway.

And some tincture of ginkgo biloba.

Helps you think straight.

Anna Thank you.

I'm actually fine but –

The Proprietor Evangeline says he's 'the one'.

She actually believes there is such a thing.

Poor naive child.

The Man Where is the climber?

The Proprietor looks through his binoculars.

The Proprietor He's on the long traverse before the second chimney.

He's making an attempt on the chimney.

At this time of year the ice is melting and the rocks come pinging down the chimney like bowling balls in an alley.

He gives The Man the binoculars.
The Man scans.

The Man I've got him.

He's on his own.

The Proprietor Solo.

The Man If he falls . . .

The Proprietor We're all on our own when we fall, pilgrim.

The Proprietor takes the binoculars back.

I need the room cleared by twelve o'clock, Miss Edwards.
  It's going to seem so quiet here when you're gone.
  After all the hustle and bustle.

The Proprietor leaves.

The Man You don't know who I am, Anna.

Anna I don't care about that.

The Man I could be anybody.

Anna I'm falling for you.

> *A pause.*
>   *Anna touches his face.*
>   *They kiss.*
>   *Briefly.*
>   *Anna stops kissing.*
>   *A pause.*
>   *Anna is a little embarrassed.*

I'd better go up to my room.
  Collect my things together.

She takes the aspirin and drinks the water.

I still have an hour or so before check-out time.
  I'll just be in my room.

> *Anna leaves.*
>   *The Man remains.*
>   *He looks at the photographs.*

The Proprietor comes out.
  He looks through the binoculars.

The Proprietor HE'S STILL ALIVE, EVANGELINE.
YOU'RE ALL RIGHT FOR NOW.

He puts the binoculars down on the table.

She wants to go to the toilet.

Can't move from the chaise longue in case she catches sight of him through the patio doors.

Where's Morgana?

The Man She said she was going to pack.

The Proprietor I've heard that one before.

The Man What do you mean?

The Proprietor 'Going to pack'.

The Man That's what she said.

The Proprietor 'Just in case you wondered where I might be.'

The Man Do you think she wants me to go up to her?

The Proprietor I'm the proprietor of a hotel, pilgrim.
I understand the psychology of these English women.
It's the same every time.
The dusk, the mountains, and always, always a pilgrim.
It's the scallop shell.
It's a powerful aphrodisiac.

The Man Maybe she just didn't want to miss check-out time.

The Proprietor Pilgrims are seekers after truth. Some people like to think they're truths waiting to be found.

The Man Do you think I should go up to her?

The Proprietor If you want to have sex? Yes.

The Man There's no need to be crude.

The Proprietor Crude.
Unsentimental.
I'm from New York.
I don't got time for bullshit.

The Man She's attractive.
  I think there's a connection between us.
  After what happened to me in the snow.
  She's damaged. Fragile.
  I want to –

The Proprietor Yes yes.
  Saddle up yo hoss, cowboy, save da lady.
  Indulge the fantasy.
  Go on.

The Man You don't think I should?

The Proprietor God's given you the soul of a child,
pilgrim.
  He's washed you clean.
  If you want to plash about in the muddy fens of sexual
desire.
  Be my guest.
  Just don't be surprised if the stains don't wash out.

The Man I don't think love has to be a staining thing.

The Proprietor You love her?

The Man I may do.

The Proprietor Ask yourself what was so intolerable that
you decided to walk across the Pyrenees in the snow,
pilgrim?
  What skin did you want to shed?
  I like you. I think of myself as your friend.
  If you start looking for yourself in her arms
  You don't know what horrors you might find.
  . . .
  Bernard-Marie's here – you need to sign your daily
sheet.

The Man Send him out.

The Proprietor You'll have to go in.
He won't come out here.
Evangeline's spooked him.
He doesn't want to see the climber fall.

The Man gets up.

The Man Listen, thanks, Pedro.
You've been very helpful.

The Proprietor Don't mind me, pilgrim.
I'm quarter Basque on my dad's side.
We're a shit-stirring people.
We like to throw spanners in works.

The Man leaves.
The Proprietor looks through the binoculars again.
Vivienne enters.

The Proprietor How's your eyesight?

Vivienne All right.
I need glasses to read.

The Proprietor There's a climber on the face.
He's solo.
Very likely to fall.
If you don't want to see a man fall.
Look away.

Vivienne I hadn't noticed.

The Proprietor puts the binoculars on the table.

The Proprietor Can I bring you anything?

Vivienne A herbal tea.

The Proprietor You look gorgeous today, Mrs
Sutherland.
The mountain air must suit you.

Vivienne Thank you.

The Proprietor You know, when you arrived,
    You struck me as elegant and dignified. A good-looking
woman.
    But you seemed weary, pale.
    These past few days you've blossomed.
    There's a bloom in your cheeks.
    Mountain air and camomile tea.

Vivienne Pedro, I'm a Scotswoman.
    You won't win my custom with flattery.
    But if you supply me with a working hairdryer socket
and clean bathroom towels I promise you, Pedro, your
name will be spoken of in whispers in all the secret places
where my countrywomen gather.

The Proprietor The handyman's on holiday.
    I'll look at it myself today.

Vivienne You said that yesterday.

The Proprietor Yes, but I mean it today.

The Proprietor leaves.
    *Vivienne looks over her shoulder to see if she can see
the climber.*
    She can't.
    She turns back.
    She puts her hand on the binoculars.
    She takes her hand from the binoculars.

The Man enters.

The Man You're back.
    Did you enjoy your walk?

Vivienne Very much.

The Man Good.
    . . .
    That's my coffee.

81

Vivienne Why don't you sit down?

He sits.

Pedro's bringing me a camomile tea.

The Man Calming.

Vivienne I find it is.

The Man A stressful time.

Vivienne For both of us.

The Man What is it you said you do, Mrs Sutherland?

Vivienne Vivienne.

The Man Vivienne.

Vivienne I'm a speech therapist.
    Was.
    I gave it up.

The Man Why?

Vivienne To look for you.

The Man I see.
    Did you enjoy speech therapy?

Vivienne Very much.
    But I wasn't unhappy to leave.
    It was quite liberating really.
    I sold the house.
    Our house.
    Made rather a lot of money.
    You were always good with property.

The Man Vivienne.
    I seem to have an accent.
    Anna – from the Consulate – she noticed.
    'A lilt,' she said.
    She couldn't place it –
    Do you . . . ?

Vivienne A lot of people confuse speech therapy with elocution . . .

The Man I know.
I know what speech therapy is.

Vivienne Of course you do.

The Man I was just asking whether you heard anything in my voice.

Vivienne You have a Scottish accent, Keith.
It's very light.
But it's there.

The Man I wondered if it might be West Country.

Vivienne No, it isn't West Country.
It's posh Edinburgh.
With a tiny amount of residual Aberdeenshire.
. . .
Your father was a schoolteacher.
He was keen you spoke properly.
When we lived in Africa, our friends were all English.
We both unconsciously tempered our accent.
But it's there.

The Man Africa?

Vivienne For a few years.
Nigeria.
Lagos.

She brings out a photograph.

That's us.
Outside Lagos Yacht Club.

He looks at the photograph.

The Man Keith's a yachtie?

Vivienne You were.
   Never had enough money to buy a boat.
   When we moved to Edinburgh.
   You tried it a couple of times.
   Gave it up.
   Took up golf.

The Man Oh God.

Vivienne Once, at a car-boot sale, you bought a pair of cross-country skis for twenty pounds. They sat in the garage for years.

The Man He sounds like a bit of a sap.

Vivienne You wanted to ski.
   I could understand that.
   I wanted to want to play the piano.
   And speak French.

The Man Do you speak French?

Vivienne *Fermez la porte, s'il vous plaît.*

   The Man laughs.

The Man Same as me.

Vivienne We bought a cottage in the Highlands.
   At weekends we would go there.
   And for a couple of weeks in the summer.
   You were fond of it.
   I kept it on.
   I couldn't bear to sell it.
   I went back last Christmas, on my own.
   I didn't know how to switch the water on.
   I had to drive to the shop and buy a crate of Evian.
   I sat by the fire and read the *Perthshire Advertiser* and –
   You see; you had always done the water.
   I did the fire, and you did the water.
   I was a bit lost without someone to do the water.

84

The Man This Keith, he sounds like –
He sounds like he should have got out more.

Vivienne It's easy to fall into habits.

The Man Still.
What a sap.
What a mediocre . . .

Something of a pause.

So according to your theory. Keith – somehow – he has
what?
An affair?

Vivienne With a stripper.

The Man Good God.

Vivienne Yes, I was somewhat taken aback by that
detail.

The Man He breaks off the affair. He fakes his own
death – he ends up wandering in the Pyrenees clutching
a scallop shell?
. . .
From what you say it doesn't sound very 'Keith'. Does
it?

Vivienne No.
But then Keith died, didn't he?
You killed him.

The Man Isn't it possible that Keith really is dead?
That he didn't fake it?
That he walked into the sea and he drowned?
Because he couldn't bear how unbelievably mediocre
he was?
How little he'd done with his life?

Vivienne We were both so innocent, Keith.
The things I've seen since – the things you've seen.

Things we didn't know before.
We've changed.
Really.

The Man How do you know what I've seen?

Vivienne I've been following you.

The Man You followed Keith?

Vivienne It took some time. After that Christmas I
decided to look for you.
    I tracked you down to the Western Isles. You were
staying on a croft on Benbecula. I found you.

    She takes out a collection of photographs.
    She puts the first one down on the table.
    He picks it up.

I watched you walking on the beach one morning, in the
wind and the rain. I remember thinking about how you'd
often said we should buy a dog. I remember thinking –
'Why don't you buy a dog, you stupid man, to walk along
that beach with you?' And I thought, 'Well, he's working
things out. He needs space to work things out.' So I didn't
confront you, I just kept an eye on you.
    The local barman phoned me every day.
    And then one day he called and said you'd disappeared
again.
    And I thought – oh no, this time he's actually walked
into the sea.
    But in fact you'd come into some money. The barman
didn't know how. But you'd gone up to Stornoway and
bought yourself a motorcycle. And you'd taken the ferry
to Ullapool. Fifteen thousand you spent on that bike.
I very near wept, because you'd had a bike when we were
courting and you'd sold it when we got married.

    She shows him another photo.

You rode that bike down the motorway, Keith, and I was driving behind you in the Volvo desperately trying to keep up. Weaving and bobbing through the traffic. I was worried you would crash.

I thought, his balance won't be good enough. He'll wobble and fall. But it was as if you'd never been off that bike, Keith.

As you drove into Fife my heart was in my mouth because I thought you were coming home.

But you turned off at Rosyth and caught the ferry to Zeebrugge.

The Man Good old Keith.
Sorry.
What happened next?

Vivienne On the ferry you fell into company with some Norwegian Hell's Angels and spent the next three months on amphetamines riding with them across Europe.

Another photo.

Torsten, Karl, Jonny, Gogoboy and Mickey Finn.
Poor Keith, you never stopped. The Norwegians and the drugs pushed you on.

More photos.

Hamburg and Berlin and Leipzig and Munich and Prague and Vienna.

The Man looks through the photos.

All the time, me following you in the old Volvo.
We took the grand tour. You stayed in the filthy city campsites and drank beer with the Angels. I stayed in B and Bs and visited cathedrals. Torsten was my spy. I begged him to keep an eye on you. I think they adopted you – the 'Old Man', they called you – '*gammle gubben*'.
You were happy.

I saw you one night sleeping with a young Slovenian girl by the fire in a campsite in Bratislava.

I couldn't bear to break your spell.

You broke away from the Hell's Angels not long after.

They stole your bike. I think there was a fight. That's how you got the cut on your forehead. A biker's chain tore your head open and they left you for dead in a hedge. I patched you up with the first-aid kit in the car and I called an ambulance. When they came to pick you up they asked me who I was and

I said I was just passing.

When you came out of hospital, the walking started. You walked through Austria, through Switzerland into France. Now you insisted on staying in the best hotels. It was easy to follow you. I would drive to the next five-star place and wait for you to turn up dusty from the road and take a room. I'd take a room next to yours.

It was late summer. You'd sit on your balcony and I'd sit on mine and together we'd watch the sunsets in the evening. You didn't know I was there, of course, but I think you sensed something – I think you sensed –

One night a hotel barman told you about the pilgrims' way to Santiago de Compostela.

And you became a pilgrim.

The Man You've had an adventure.

Vivienne It had to stop eventually.

The Man Keith, who'd have thought it?

Vivienne I think you sensed something.
I think that's why you became a pilgrim.

The Man Sensed what?

Vivienne I'm ill, Keith.
I'm not well.

Something of a pause.

I've been angry, and sad . . .
Scared, very scared sometimes.
I've spent the night with conference delegates
And
Yet – there has been lightness, Keith. Joy, even. In
moments.
Everything I was has fallen away from me.
My house, my work, my friends, my life.
Even the old Volvo died at the foot of the valley.
All that's left of me is here.
And I still . . .
You're the only person I have, Keith.
We shaped ourselves around each other.
If that's what love is.
I love you.
. . .
I don't know any other way to say it.

The Man This Keith.
This man Keith.
You . . .
The way he's behaved.

Vivienne I know, it's silly, isn't it?

The Man You never abandoned him.

Vivienne Perhaps I should have.

The Man Why didn't you?

Vivienne I have nowhere to go back to.

The Man I do sense something from you, Vivienne.

The Man looks at Vivienne.

There's an undertow.
It's – (*The Man tries very hard to identify what he is
feeling.*) There isn't a word for it I can think of in
English.

It reminds me of the snow.
The snow.

Something of a pause.

The Proprietor enters.
  He is carrying a pot of camomile tea.
  He puts the tea on the table.
  He picks up the binoculars.

The Proprietor STILL ALIVE, EVANGELINE.
WAIT. HOLD ON!
. . .
NO! JUST A WOBBLE. YOU'RE ALL RIGHT. HE'S
FINE.
There's your tea.

Vivienne You took your time.

The Proprietor That'll be your hairdryer socket fixed.
And Evangeline's seen to the bathroom for you.

Vivienne Thank you.

The Proprietor No need to thank me.
If people moan about something,
I take action.
Most of my customers are moany old cows.
So, you know,
It's better to pander to their whims.
Keeps them off my back.

Vivienne puts some money on the table.
  Anna enters.
  She has a very small suitcase.

Thank you, madam.

Vivienne You're welcome, Pedro.

The Proprietor takes the money.
  He returns inside.

Anna Hello, Mrs Sutherland.

Vivienne Hello, Anna.

The Man Come and join us.

Something of a pause.
Anna comes over to the table.
Pulls up a chair.
Sits.

Vivienne Tell me, Anna, in your room, does the hairdryer socket work?

Anna Yes.

Vivienne Ah.

Anna Why?

Vivienne Just something I've got going with Pedro.

Anna touches her hair.

Anna I ought to be leaving soon.

Vivienne Is it a long journey?

Anna A fairly long journey.

The Man To Marseilles.

Anna Back to – all the usual.

Anna laughs.
Something of a pause.

Vivienne Keith said you'd noticed his accent.

Anna Who?

Vivienne Keith.

The Man I mentioned it.

Anna Did you?

Vivienne He did. It's Scottish.

Anna Don't worry. We'll be sending the tape to experts in London.
  So it should all be cleared up then.

The Man You did say you needed to interview Vivienne.

Anna Yes. I do. Just routine. For the records.

The Man Would you like me to . . . ?

Anna Yes, if you don't mind.

The Man I'll just – I'll just go and say hello to Bernard-Marie.
  Do you mind if I take these photographs.

Vivienne Not at all.

The Man He's depressed.
  Don't tell him I told you.
  I'll just –
  Some of these pictures will give him a laugh.
  This one with the beard.
  I'll just see if I can
  Cheer him up.

  The Man leaves.
    Something of a pause.

Anna So.

  Anna opens her little suitcase.
    Takes out her tape recorder.
    She puts it on the table.

Last night, you gave me your file on your husband.
  Thank you for that.
  I'll send that back to England with the other material.
  I'm sure it'll be given due consideration.
  All I need now is to take a short statement from you.
  . . .
  Before I switch this on.

Off the record.
Mrs Sutherland.
What's your game?

Vivienne I'm sorry?

Anna I think you know what I'm talking about.

Vivienne I don't understand.

Anna You're here. You're watching him. He has money.
You don't say anything and then last night – just when
you've gathered enough information you –
Move in.
So what's your game?

Vivienne Is this the interview?

Anna Never mind what it is.
Answer the question.

Vivienne He's my husband.

Anna Really?

Vivienne I have photographs.

Anna We all have photographs, don't we?

Vivienne I don't know what you mean.

Anna Computers.
We all have photographs of ourselves next to . . .
whoever we want.

Anna takes a photograph out of her filofax.

Here's me with Bill Clinton. So don't give me
photographs.

Anna puts the photograph back.

Vivienne That man is Keith Sutherland.
I know my husband.

93

Anna There's no point lying, because this is all going to be verified by experts.

Vivienne He's Keith.

Anna I don't know what you expected, Mrs Sutherland.
Some idiot, perhaps.
But you've got me.
And I don't believe you.
And even if I did believe you.
Even if you were married to him.
He's changed. He's . . . new.
What's your game?
Did you come back to see what you'd done?
Flying in here like a raven.
To peck over his bones.
You vampire.
I sense people and I sensed you the moment I saw you –
I smelled blood.

Vivienne I'm not entirely certain that a British diplomat ought to be talking to a British citizen with quite your tone.

Anna Tone? Whose tone? Mine – what about yours?
Winding me up.
Talking about my hair.
Setting the proprietor onto me.
I've watched every step you've taken.
I'm onto you.

Vivienne I don't need to sit and listen to this.

Vivienne is about to rise.

Anna Stay there, you old witch.
I found him first.
And he likes me.
And you can't bear that, can you?
Seeing chances slip away time after time?

Back against the wall to stop you falling down.
Looking out at the dancers like Medusa.
Cold stare.
Turning everything into stone.
Every man you touch goes cold on you.
Well, I'm out on the parquet, witch.
Whirling about,
And you can't bear to see me.
You just can't bear it.

Vivienne stands.

Vivienne I think you should be aware, Miss Edwards,
I will be talking to the Consul about this.

Anna Your perfume.
Do you smear it on or what?
Cloying. Roses.
My mother used to wear that perfume.
It's actually overwhelming.
It's – overpowering –

Anna pauses.

Could you put me on the floor, please?
Could you loosen my top?
Would you mind?

Anna's left arm begins to jerk uncontrollably.
  Anna's face becomes blank.
  She is about to slump.
  Vivienne catches her.

Vivienne Are you all right?

. . .

Miss Edwards?

Vivienne puts Anna on the floor.
  Anna's arm continues to jerk, rhythmically.
  Vivienne pauses.

PEDRO!

Vivienne loosens Anna's top button.
  Anna's arm continues to jerk.
  Vivienne watches.
  The Proprietor and The Man enter.
  They see what's happening.
  Anna's arm stops jerking.
  Stillness.

The Man What's wrong with her?

The Proprietor kneels.
  Puts his hand on her lips.

The Proprietor She's breathing.

Vivienne I think she's had a fit.

The Man She said, she told me she was epileptic.

The Proprietor Stand back. Let her breathe.
  Get me a cushion.

*Vivienne takes off her jacket, folds it up to make a
pillow.. She puts it under Anna's head.*
  Anna opens her eyes.

Anna Thank you.

. . .

  The sun's in my eyes.

She shields her eyes.

I'm terribly sorry if I've caused any embarrassment.
  I appear to have had a fit.
  How long was I out?

Vivienne Only moments.

Anna Could somebody hold me?

Vivienne takes Anna's arm.
  Anna gets to her feet. Slowly.

Vivienne Slowly.
  Sit her down.

  Anna sits.

Anna Please don't be alarmed.
  I know what's happened and why.
  I'm sorry if my behaviour was erratic immediately
before I fitted.
  That happens.
  I do apologise if I did anything embarrassing.

Vivienne Don't. Please. Don't worry.

  *Vivienne sits, opposite Anna, puts her hand on Anna's
  hand.*

Anna It's entirely my own fault.
  The hangover.
  I pushed myself beyond a limit.
  I should have known better.

The Proprietor Can I bring you anything?
  Water?
  A doctor?

Anna No.
  I'll just sit here for a moment.
  If that's all right.

The Proprietor Of course.

Anna Could you take my things back to my room?
  Would you mind?
  I don't think I can travel to Marseilles today.
  I'll travel tommorow.

The Proprietor Certainly, Miss Edwards.
  And, Miss Edwards.
  There will be no charge.

  The Proprietor whispers something to Keith.

The Proprietor leaves, taking Anna's suitcase with him.

The tape recorder and the binoculars remain on the table.

Vivienne's hand remains on Anna's hand.

Vivienne How are you feeling?

Anna Tired.

Vivienne Perhaps you should lie down.

Anna In a moment.
It's a beautiful afternoon.
You're very kind, Vivienne.
Can you smell the thaw?
Gorgeous.

The Man What was it like?

Anna The usual.
Terribly dark.
Then clear.
Then nothing – which is the opposite of nothing.
Then gorgeous.
Then sad.

The Man Gorgeous.

Anna Now, it's sad. Only now.

The Man Did you sense –? Did you have a sense of –?

Anna Yes.

The Man Maybe that is what happened to me in the snow.
What happened to you.

Anna A fit.

The Man Maybe.

Vivienne I think Anna has had enough questions.
Don't you, Keith?

The Man Yes. I'm sorry.

Anna What did Pedro say to you?

The Man He said . . .
I'm not sure if you –

Anna Tell me.

The Man He said you were a visitor from the world of
spirits.
You could bring us good luck or bad luck.
We had to placate you with gifts.

Anna laughs.

Anna I'm going to go up to my room now.
To lie down.
That's where I'll be.
If anyone wants to find me.

Anna leaves.
The Man sits.
*Anna, just as she is about to exit, looks back at The
Man.*
The Man is looking at her.
She exits.

Vivienne Poor girl.

The Man Poor girl.

Vivienne Well,
My bathroom's clean, or so I'm told.
I'm going to wash, and rest.
Perhaps you'd like to join me for dinner.

The Man I need to think.
Maybe I should go for a walk.

A walk up through the pines.
By the burn.

Vivienne Perhaps you'd like to join me for dinner, after your walk.

The Man I should go to her.

Vivienne You must do what you think is best.

The Man A walk up through the pines.
By the burn.

A pause.
Vivienne makes to leave.
The Man remains still, looking away from her.
He begins to cry.
The following words are a response to his tears and each word provokes tears.

The Man Burn.
Burn.
Burn.
It's such a gorgeous word, Viv.
Burn.
She's . . . I've . . .
Burn.
. . .
What would Keith do in this situation?

Vivienne Keith walked into the sea.

Vivienne leaves.
The Man presses play on the tape recorder.

The tape recorder: 'Five languages and it doesn't make sense in any of them.'
The smallest of laughs.

He rewinds.
Presses play again.

The tape recorder: 'Five languages and it doesn't make sense in any of them.'
    The smallest of laughs.

The Proprietor comes out.

The Proprietor Why didn't you tell me she was a spirit?
    For God's sake, pilgrim.
    You've visited the realm of angels.
    You must have spotted it.

The Man I sensed something.

The Proprietor You don't fuck about with the spirits.
    Jesus. Don't you know anything?
    We could be in big trouble.
    This is an avalanche-prone area, you know.
    Good God.
    You could have landed us right in it.

The Man I'm sorry.

The Proprietor It's too late for sorry now.

The Proprietor looks through the binoculars.

Damn.
    I knew it.
    I can't find him.
    Damn.

The Man The climber.

The Proprietor He's not there.

The Man Maybe he's reached the summit.

The Proprietor It's nearly dark.
    Oh God.
    Look.
    This is all your fault.
    Don't tell Evangeline. It'll kill her.
    You don't want that on your conscience as well.

The Man I'm sorry, Pedro.
   I'm really sorry.

The Proprietor OK. This is what we do.
   We tell Evangeline he reached the summit.
   OK.
   But before he left he told us he had to go back to
Germany.
   Right.
   He told us to tell Evangeline he loved her.
   But he'd lied.
   And he was married.
   And he had to go back.
   And he loved her so much he couldn't bear to tell her.
   But he waved, from the summit.
   We saw him wave.
   That's what we tell Evangeline.

The Man What if he did reach the summit?

The Proprietor Then he can do what the fuck he wants.

The Man Evangeline will know we've lied.

The Proprietor You and your sorry conscience.
   Learn – idiot.
   Carry the lie.
   Put the stone in the old rucksack and add it to the rest.
   Good God.
   There's no vanity like an Englishman's concern for his
conscience.
   Let the poor girl pick up her own stones when her time
comes.
   I live in the mountains, pilgrim.
   We've all been in the snow.
   You're not so special.
   Not round here.

   The Proprietor leaves.

The Man picks up the binoculars.
He looks through them.
Anna enters.

Anna You didn't come.

The Man No.

Anna I hoped you –

The Man I know.

Anna I need to know where we stand.

The Man I see.

. . .

Sit down, Anna.

Anna doesn't sit down.
Something of a pause.

I like you, Anna.

Anna Come to Marseilles with me.

The Man Anna, I'm . . .

Anna You're what? What are you?

The Man I'm . . .

Anna Come with me.

The Man I'm too old for you.
I'm a damp towel over a flame.

Anna I see.

The Man You're so alive.
We made a connection.
I even love you. In a way.
But it's impossible.

Anna Do you know how tiring it is?
Sensing?

Moving back and forth between worlds?
How it wears you down?

The Man No.

Anna Waking up from that, so many times, back to this?

The Man No.

Anna No. Of course you don't.
You've only done it once.

The Man I'm sorry.

Anna You could have come with me.
You could.

The Man I'm too afraid.

Anna Yes.

The Man I'm too weak.

Anna Yes.

The Man It's my fault I –

Something of a pause.

Would you like to join us for dinner?
It's a lovely evening.

Anna No thank you.
I'm quite tired.
I need to sleep.
After a fit I tend to sleep very deeply, for a long time.
If you could ask Mrs Sutherland to send a statement to
Marseilles.
That would be quite helpful to me.

The Man I will.

Anna What happened to the climber?

The Man He made the summit.
  I saw him waving.

Anna I'm glad.

The Man Yes.

Anna Well.
  Goodnight.
  I won't see you in the morning.

  Something of a pause.
    Anna leaves.

The Man You've forgotten your tape recorder.

  Anna comes back.
    She picks up the tape recorder.
    She takes the tape out.
    She stands on it.
    Stamps it into small pieces.

Won't the experts need that?

Anna You don't need an expert to tell you who you are.
  You know who you are.
  You live with it.

  Anna leaves.
    The Man remains.
    The Man rises from the seat.
    He goes to the edge of the terrace.
    He lights a cigarette.

  The Proprietor enters.
    As he speaks he puts a tablecloth over the table.
    He puts a candle down.
    He lights it.
    He puts down a bottle of wine and two glasses.

The Proprietor Beautiful evening.

The Man Gorgeous.

The Proprietor Warm still.

The Man Yes.

The Proprietor It's veal tonight.
Do you like veal?

The Man I don't know.

The Proprietor I love it, myself.
But then I'm Spanish.
I'll eat anything that bleeds.

The Proprietor leaves.
As he leaves he passes Vivienne entering.
Vivienne is wearing an evening dress and climbing
boots.

The Proprietor wolf-whistles.

It is now night.
The Man turns round and sees her.

Vivienne I left my heels in the Volvo.
I kept the dress.
Don't know why.

The Man It suits you.

She approaches him and stands beside him.

Vivienne It's warm tonight. The snow's melting.
The pass will be open soon.

The Man I'd like to see the pass. Everything above the
forest has been hidden in cloud since I got here. The
cloud never seems to rise.

Vivienne It will.

The Proprietor switches on the coloured lights.

The Man I was never at sea, was I?

Vivienne No.

The Man No.

Vivienne You had a cousin.

The Man A cousin?

Vivienne He had a fishing boat.

The Man Oh.

Vivienne Up near Peterhead.

The Man A cousin.

Vivienne But not you. You were never at sea.

The Man Poor Keith.

> *She holds her hand out.*
> *He takes her hand.*
> *They are quite self-conscious about it.*

Vivienne Poor Keith.

> *Music comes on: 'A Whiter Shade of Pale', Procul
> Harum.*
> *A moment between them of embarrassment.*

The Man Did Keith like this song?

Vivienne I don't think so. I don't know. He never said.

The Man I like this song.

> *There is a moment in which they experience many
> emotions.*
> *None of which they express.*

> *The moment passes.*

It would have been nice if there could have been dolphins.

> *The End.*